The Book for Every Reference Shelf

HOW TO ACHIEVE COMPETENCE IN ENGLISH is practical and concise. It contains entries as specific as bibliography, colons, envelopes, footnotes, prefixes, and roots of words, as well as comprehensive articles on broader subjects:

- how to avoid clichés
- restrictive and nonrestrictive clauses
- mnemonic devices
- poetry
- proofreading
- gerunds
- transitions
- participial phrases
- and much more.

Whether you're writing a speech, a business letter, or your thesis, this book provides quick answers on dozens of topics—and gives you all the tools you need to communicate and compete successfully!

Clear, complete, convenient, HOW TO ACHIEVE COMPETENCE IN ENGLISH is the best language handbook you can buy.

How to Achieve Competence in English

New Revised Edition

A Quick-Reference Handbook

Eric W. Johnson

BANTAM BOOKS

NEW YORK • TORONTO • LONDON • SYDNEY • AUCKLAND

HOW TO ACHIEVE COMPETENCE IN ENGLISH:
A QUICK REFERENCE HANDBOOK

A Bantam Book/December 1976
Bantam revised edition/November 1991

ISBN 0-553-29274-9

Published simultaneously in the United States and Canada

Bantam Books are published by Bantam Books, a division of
Bantam Doubleday Dell Publishing Group, Inc. Its trade-
mark, consisting of the words "Bantam Books" and the por-
trayal of a rooster, is Registered in U.S. Patent and Trademark
Office and in other countries. Marca Registrada. Bantam
Books, 666 Fifth Avenue, New York, New York 10103.

PRINTED IN THE UNITED STATES OF AMERICA

OPM 0 9 8 7 6 5 4 3 2 1

Dedicated to

E. B. White, whose masterful writing and whose *Elements of Style* (which grew out of the work of Professor William Strunk, Jr.) have inspired in me a reverence for language and its niceties;

and

John E. Warriner, whose *English Grammar and Composition,* first course through complete course, have greatly strengthened the systematic, thorough part of my teaching of English for thirty-five years in public and independent schools.

Preface

Achieving Competence

The title of this book is *How to Achieve Competence in English*. Please note the verb *achieve*. English is a complex, wonderful, rich, rewarding subject and activity. And you don't just magically arrive at a state of competence in English. You have to achieve it! That means work, practice, accomplishment, and even play: books well read, speeches well made, compositions well written, discussions well participated in—even good marks in school and college and praise and satisfaction on the job.

Topics Covered

How to Achieve Competence in English is concise and practical, with more emphasis on practice than theory. It is not a course of study, but it backs up all courses of study. It contains no "exercises," but it helps its users exercise their English better in real life. It contains entries as specific as "bibliographies," "colons," "letters," "footnotes," "prefixes," "roots of words," "spelling demons," and "note-taking." It also contains longer articles on subjects such as debating and persuading, writing compositions, figurative language, interviewing, plays, speech-making, proofreading, taking tests and exams, vocabulary development, the origins and richness of English, and study skills. Flip through the pages and you'll see.

Preface

The Index

This is a rare book in that it contains no table of contents. Its subjects, big and small, are arranged in alphabetical order. They are also labeled by *topic numbers*—360 of them. The most important tool for using the book is the Index. The entries are all identified by topic numbers, *not* page numbers, and this makes it very easy to locate exactly what you need when you need it. Look at the Index now.

Cross-references

During or at the end of many of the alphabetically-arranged sections of the book are cross-references. Example: Topic number 80 is **Interviewing.** You'll see that there are four cross-references in the article, printed thus: COMPOSITIONS, 40; REPORTS, 130; NOTE-TAKING, 95; and FOOTNOTES, 62. You don't have to turn to the cross-references, for the article can stand on its own, but they are often helpful and always very easy to find.

Special Notes for Different Users of This Book

- *To High School and College Students*

    This book contains the basic information you need to write, read, and speak English correctly and well. It helps you deal with all your language work at school as you proceed through the curriculum, not just in English classes but in all subjects in which you need to read, write, and speak.

    How will this handbook help you at school and college? If you find that a language question arises while you are working on a lesson or a project, you can quickly look up the answer and get on with your work. You won't have to bother your teacher or instructor or wait until the teacher has time to help

Preface

you. The contents are carefully chosen to enable you to deal with the curriculum of your school—the lessons, the textbooks, the workbooks, the work sheets, the research questions. (Of course, you shouldn't use it during tests! But it *does* help you study for and take tests and exams successfully.)

At home, *How to Achieve Competence* enables you to do a better job with homework, reading books, and writing papers. It reminds you of the correct ways to do things that you've been taught in class but may have forgotten. It will also help you to go ahead of the school or college lesson plans. It will teach you what you need that hasn't yet come up in the year's work.

I hope you will discover that this book makes you a stronger, abler user of language, a better student at school and college, and a more competent citizen of the world.

- *To Teachers and Instructors*

The purpose of this book is to provide the material that enables students to do language arts work on their own in any subject. They can easily find what they need to know *now* while doing homework, writing a paper, or puzzling over a question in class. *How to Achieve Competence* will help make them more efficient studiers and test-takers. The book does not interfere with schools' planned curricula; rather, it empowers students to learn the most possible from the curriculum and to become competent users of the English language in school, at home, and out in the community.

The book saves *you* time, and it facilitates your job by making students self-sufficient, enabling them to answer questions on their own rather than having to raise their hands, interrupt class, and ask you. It

Preface

puts students on their own but in a way that is consistent with the planned curriculum of your institution. It enables you to be a better, less-pressured teacher and your students to be abler writers, readers, and speakers. And thus, teachers, principals, and even superintendents and presidents, you may want to save money and improve education by making a copy of *How to Achieve Competence in English* available to every one of your students so that they won't be dependent on those expensive learning programs, so full of day-by-day apparatus.

Also, teachers and instructors will doubtless find in the book some good ideas for teaching. Feel free to appropriate them as your own. The articles on DISCUSSIONS, 54 and MARKS, 88 are examples.

- *To Parents*

This book will enable your children to do their homework better, to use the resources in the home (including you) and in the community better. It reinforces the lessons that students are learning at school or at college. It can fill in the gaps from previous years and develop self-competence—*and* self-confidence. (You may even want to take a copy to work!)

- *To the General Reader*

Language—in your case, most likely English—is an amazing human endowment. The better we all use it, the more fun we have in life, the better we do at home or on the job, and the more we enjoy our relationships with all the people we know. I'm not saying that footnotes, spelling demons, or even participles, along with over 300 other topics, by themselves, save our marriages or make us Presidents (oops!—a cliché), but they can make us more enjoyable and enjoying people. That's not bad for a book that is only 224 pages long, and weighs only 4.43 ounces, and costs far less than an entrée at a decent restaurant.

Eric W. Johnson

Eric W. Johnson

A

1. Abbreviations

An abbreviation of a word is a shortening of it, as *prep.* for *preposition* or *Dr.* for *Doctor.* Abbreviations are followed by a period.

A common writing error is to overabbreviate. You will not go too far wrong if you avoid abbreviations except where they are conventional, as *Dr., Mr., Mrs.,* names of states in addresses, *A.M., P.M.,* and the like. (See STATE ABBREVIATIONS, 151.)

2. Accent marks   See DICTIONARIES, 52 E.

3. Acronyms

An acronym is a word formed from the first one or two letters of a number of words.

Examples:
NATO (North Atlantic Treaty Organization); UNICEF (United Nations International Children's Emergency Fund; NASA (National Aeronautics and Space Administration); TGIF (Thank God It's Friday).

> NOTE: It can be fun to make an acronym for a set of words people are using and see if they can guess it. For example: AFFAL (Acronyms for fun and laughs); AJAH (All Jane's awful habits); SIBTOH (School is better than our house). Also, making up an acronym may help you to remember a list of places, streets, or names:

PASTA (Price, Adams, Spruce, Thompson, Ardleigh).

4. Addresses

In writing out addresses, every item after the first is enclosed by commas.

Example:

My uncle lives at 3752 Chunk Street, Peach Bottom, Pennsylvania 17563, where he has a small business.

> NOTE: There is no comma between the state and the zip-code number; a comma is placed at the end of the address (unless it comes at the end of a sentence, in which case the period takes its place). For addresses in letters and on envelopes, see LETTERS, 84, and ZIP CODES, 174.

5. Adjectives

An adjective is a word used to modify NOUNS, 96 or PRONOUNS, 119. (See also MODIFIERS, 93.) It is one of the PARTS OF SPEECH, 107. It often answers the questions *what kind?* (descriptive adjective), *which one?* or *how many?* or *how much?*

Examples:

1. The *green* soup was *disgusting*. (what kind?)

2. She looked at *that* boy with interest. (which one?)

3. *Five* geniuses made *several* errors. (how many? how much?)

4. The house looks *spooky*. (what kind?)

Adjectives telling *what kind* can be compared (see COMPARISON OF ADJECTIVES AND ADVERBS, 37).

6. Adverbs

An adverb is a word used to modify a VERB, 168; ADJECTIVE, 5; or another adverb. (See also MODIFIERS, 93.) It is one of the PARTS OF SPEECH, 107. Most adverbs modify verbs. An adverb often answers the question *how?*, *where?*, *when?*, or *to what extent?*

Examples:

1. He ate *enthusiastically*. (how?)

2. She *calmly* pushed him into the pool. (how?)

3. He sank *there*. (where?)

4. The paper arrived *late*. (when?)

5. *Yesterday* my mother had a fit. (when?)

6. Please *never* eat rabbit in my house. (to what extent?)

7. The speaker droned on *forever*. (to what extent?)

NOTE: Many adverbs are simply a combination of an ADJECTIVE and the ending *-ly*: *bright* (adj.), *brightly* (adv.); *calm, calmly*. Such adverbs generally answer the question *how?* and can be compared.

7. Agreement of pronouns and antecedents

A PRONOUN, 119 must always agree with the NOUN, 96 that precedes (goes before) it, the ANTECEDENT, 16.

Example:

John loves his mother. But she

sometimes criticizes him too even much and then

he forgets his love for her. But it comes back.

A

8. Agreement of subjects and verbs

SUBJECTS, 153 and VERBS, 168 must agree in number in all SENTENCES, 139: that is, if the subject is singular, the singular form of the verb must be used; if plural, plural. (*Singular* means one only; *plural* means more than one.)

Examples:

1. The *pupils* all *sleep* during class.
   (plural subject) (plural verb)

2. *One* of the boys *beats*
   (singular subject) (singular verb)
   up weaklings.

3. *He* *doesn't* like it.
   (singular subject) (singular verb)

9. Alliteration

Alliteration means the repetition of the first letter or sound in a group of words, especially in POETRY, 114.

Examples:

1. The sun sank slowly.
2. George gazed at gorgeous girls.

10. All right

One of the most commonly misspelled items in the English language is *all right*. Remember: This expression is *never* correct as one word, *alright* (No!). It is always two words.

11. A lot

Another even more commonly misspelled item is *a lot*. Remember: It is *never* correct as one word, *alot*. It is always two words: *a lot*.

> NOTE: There is an English word *allot*. Look it up in one of your DICTIONARIES, 52.

4

12. Alphabet

If you don't know your alphabet (from the Greek *alpha* [a], *beta* [b], etc.), learn it—all the way down to *Z*. To find a word in a DICTIONARY, 52, or even in this book, knowing the alphabet is essential. A good way to memorize it is to learn it according to the well-known tune of "Twinkle, Twinkle, Little Star," thus:

ABCDEF*G*
HIJKLMNO*P*
Q and R and S and *T*,
UVWXYZ.
That's the alphabet, you see,
And it goes from A to Z.

You need, also, to learn how to alphabetize words (place them in alphabetical order) down to the second, third, or fourth letters: c u c umber, c u d, c u d d le, c u d g el.

13. Among, between

Use *among* when referring to more than two things or people. Use *between* when referring to only two.

Examples:
1. There was a rock *between* Jesse and Joan.
2. Albert is uncomfortable *among* strangers.

14. Analogies

An analogy is a comparison between two or more people, things, or subjects.

Examples:
1. Our teacher is sometimes like a devil, but more often like a strict angel.
2. My pile of dirty socks is worse than smelly garbage.
3. Writing by hand is torture, but typing is a breeze.

A

15. Announcements See SPEECH-MAKING, 146

16. Antecedents

An antecedent is the noun (or nouns) to which a pronoun refers.

Example:

George likes books. He likes them so much that he hardly ever watches TV. (*George* and *books* are the antecedents of *he* and *them,* respectively.)

17. Antonyms

An antonym is a word that is opposite in meaning to another word:

Examples:
good, bad; sad, happy; stupid, intelligent

18. Apostrophes

A. The apostrophe indicates possession, the possessive CASE, 32.
   1. When the possessive noun is singular, add *'s.* (The *cat's* collar is too tight.); (The *girl's* dress is short.); (My mother-in-law's words are often wise.)
   2. When the possessive noun is plural and ends in *s,* add the apostrophe only. (*Girls'* sports deserve facilities equal to *boys'.*)
   3. When the possessive noun is plural and does not end in *s,* add *'s.* (The *men's, women's,* and *children's* shouts brought the police.)
   4. If the possessive noun is singular and ends in *s,* add either *'s* or *'* only. (*Charles's* tonsils were larger than *Mrs. Jones's.*) Or: (*Charles'* Honda was faster than *Mr. Jones'* tricycle.)

   NOTE: Except for *one's,* possessive pronouns use no apostrophe (*hers, its, ours, yours,* etc.).

6

B. A second use for the apostrophe is to show that a word has been contracted or shortened. Use an apostrophe in a CONTRACTION, 43 at the place where letters or numbers have been omitted.
   1. *Music's* the medicine of a troubled mind. (Music is)
   2. Please *don't* eat the daisies. (do not)
   3. Good *mornin'!* (*g* omitted)
   4. Class of *'72* (19 omitted from 1972)

19. Appendices

An appendix is a supplementary section following the main text of a book or article. It gives extra information: maps, tables, charts, copies of documents, etc. When there is more than one appendix, the term *appendices* (or *appendixes*) is used.

20. Appositives

An appositive is a word or phrase within a sentence that follows a noun and gives information about it. Appositives are set off by commas.

Examples:
1. This handbook, *a dull but useful volume,* should not be burned at the end of the year.
2. Fido's barking awoke Smirk, *the neighborhood grouch.*

When appositives are short and there is no pause before them, use no commas.

Examples:
1. The painter *Michelangelo* ate clams.
2. His daughter Julie was gorgeous.

   NOTE: A group of words that begins with *who* or *which* is not an appositive but a CLAUSE, 33. It contains a subject and a verb; an appositive does not.

Example:

Sara Ogle,	*who arrived late,*	was spurned.
	(a clause, not an appositive)	

21. Articles

The words *a, an,* and *the* are PARTS OF SPEECH, 107, called articles. They are the most frequently used ADJECTIVES, 5.

22. Asterisks (*)

An asterisk (*) is often used to refer to a FOOTNOTE, 62 at the bottom (foot) of the page.

Example:
*Michael's wife** was always ready to . . .

---

*The former Rachel Rock, a famous orator.

B

23. Bibliographies

In writing REPORTS, 130, you will probably use many sources, including television, newspapers, films, or personal interviews, though books and magazines are usually the most commonly used. At the end of the paper you should list your sources in a *bibliography,* arranged alphabetically by each author's last name. Each entry in a bibliography should include information about the author, title, place of publication, publisher, and date of publication of your source. For magazines and newspapers, specify the title of the article you read, and if there is one, list the volume number of the publication from which this article is drawn after you write the name of the publication.While there are a number of acceptable ways of listing information in a bibliography, the following is perhaps the most common:

book: Mailer, Norman. *The Fight.* Boston: Little, Brown and Company, 1975.

magazine: Dubrow, Marsha. "Female Assertiveness: How a Pussycat Can Learn to Be a Panther." *New York Magazine,* July 28, 1975.

NOTE: Titles of books and names of magazines are underlined (italicized); titles of articles or chapters in magazines or books are enclosed in quotation marks.

B

24. Black (or African-American) English

Black English is a dialect of English spoken by some African-Americans. While many people, including many Blacks, have considered it substandard English (see NON-STANDARD ENGLISH, 94), in fact, it is a dialect of English. Much in Black English that seems to Americans who don't know the dialect to be grammatically incorrect is actually a consistent application of African principles of language structure. It is often more difficult for those who speak Black English to speak STANDARD ENGLISH, 150, the dialect that most Americans, including many African-Americans, use and the one in which all basic school and college texts are written. In a sense, therefore, to do well in the workplace, African-Americans have to become bi-dialectical: to speak both Black English and standard English.

25. Book reports

Book reports have several uses: to provide a record of your reading; to share information and opinions about books with your classmates; to keep your teacher informed about your independent reading; to provide subjects for original writing based on a book but drawing on your own thoughts and experiences as you discuss its subject matter, ideas, style, plot (if any), characters, setting, strengths and weaknesses, and so forth.

A simple, very useful book report can be done on a single page of a notebook or on a five-by-eight-inch index card, which can be posted or filed for sharing with classmates. Here is an example:

Author: Mike Littwin
Title: ¡Fernando!
Publisher, etc.: Bantam, New York, © 1981, 117 pages
Difficulty rating: easy
Enjoyment rating: quite enjoyable

Brief summary (25–50 words to inform prospective readers and your teacher): Tells the life history and amazing performance of L.A. Dodgers pitcher Fernando Valenzuela. He reached the U.S. major leagues from Mexico at age twenty and even had lunch with President Reagan. Lots of facts and personal stories. Fifty pages in English, fifty pages in Spanish translation.

My reaction (25–50 words giving your opinion of the book and why you liked or disliked it): I liked the factual reporting and the amazingly fast way young Fernando rose to the top. Also, it's a valuable book for Spanish-speaking readers. Somewhat brief and superficial, but fun to read.

26. Book reviews

Most major newspapers and magazines publish reviews of books they think are important and of interest to readers. The Sunday editions of newspapers are most likely to carry reviews. In order for you to decide whether or not to buy, borrow from a library, or read a book, it is often useful to read a review of it first. If you do, notice who wrote the review and whether you think the reviewer's opinion is worthy of respect. Sometimes a good book review will give the essence of the book and make it unnecessary for you to read it.

Be cautious about brief quotes from reviews printed on book jackets or at the front or back of the book. For instance, a quote might read: "Full of humor and excitement" but omit the remainder of the sentence: "but superficial and containing so many serious errors that it cannot be recommended."

27. Books

The world's best teaching machines are books. They are compact, convenient, durable, comparatively inexpensive, and don't get out of order. The American writer Jesse Lee Bennett said, "Books are the compasses and telescopes and sextants and charts ... to help us navigate the dangerous seas of human life." Here a few facts that will enable you to navigate the contents of books.

A. *The table of contents*

At the front of most nonfiction and some works of fiction there is a table of contents listing the titles of sections and chapters of the book. Reading it will give you an overview of the book, help you decide whether it is one you want or need to read, and show how the various parts of the book fit into the whole.

B. *The index*

Nonfiction books often end with an index, which is simply an alphabetical list of topics, subjects, and names covered in the text. If you need to know whether a specific piece of information can be found in a book, or where to find it, use the index.

C. *Preface, introduction, or foreword*

Many books open with a preface, introduction, or foreword in which the author explains the nature of the book, his or her purpose in writing it, and the readers for whom he or she thinks it will be of value. Although such a judgment of the value of the book may not be entirely objective, what the author says may help you benefit from the book—or may even make you decide not to read it.

D. *Title page and copyright notice*

At the very front of the book is the *title page*, which lists the title, author, and publisher of the book. On the back of this page is the copyright date—given when the book was finished and sent to the Library of Congress (for books published in the U.S.A.) for copyrighting. It will probably look like this: © 1987. Sometimes there are several dates, the latest one being that of the most recent revision, major or minor. It is often important to know when a book was written so that you can tell whether the information in it is up-to-date. (See also COPYRIGHT, 45.)

28. Brackets ([ ])

A. Brackets indicate that your own words are inserted or substituted within a quotation.

Example:
Samuel Johnson wrote in 1775: "There is now less flogging in our great schools than formerly,—but then less is learned there, so that what the boys get [win] at one end they lose at the other."

B. Brackets indicate a parenthetical expression within a set of PARENTHESES, 105.

Example:
The King James Version of the Bible (provided in most hotel rooms by Gideons International [see the article on page 356] is written in the English of the seventeenth century.

Be sure not to use brackets instead of parentheses.

29. Brainstorming

Brainstorming means thinking freely, often in a group, about a topic or problem and writing down all ideas that come to mind, no matter how crazy they may seem. Brainstorming may be a good way to get started on a writing or speaking project. Jot down everything, and then look over the jottings and make some decisions.

A difficulty some people have in getting started on a project is that they want to have what is exactly perfect straight from their heads. When this doesn't happen, they get stuck. *Suggestion:* Just start! Write and write! *Then* you can go back and see what you've got. It may, with editing, be a very good paper or speech.

30. Bring, take

Use *bring* when the act is *toward* the speaker.

B

Examples:
1. Bring that chewing gum to me, please, and then throw it in the wastebasket.
2. Please bring me two pizzas and four milk shakes.

Use *take* when the act is *away from* the speaker.

Examples:
1. Take that cat out of the house.
2. When you leave, please take your old clothes with you.

C

31. Capitalization

In general, capitalize: (a) the first word of any sentence; (b) the pronoun *I;* and (c) any proper noun—that is, any word that is a name: "Mississippi," "Bob." It is also important to know when *not* to capitalize.

A. *When to capitalize*
1. Capitalize the names of months, days of the week, and holidays (but *not* the names of the four seasons).

   Examples:

December	spring
April	summer
Tuesday	autumn, fall
Saturday	winter
Easter	
Washington's Birthday	

2. Capitalize the names of particular organizations, schools, colleges, universities, buildings, and companies.

   Examples:
   the International Red Cross
   Central High School
   City University of New York
   the Philadelphia Mint
   Potomac Electric Company

3. Capitalize the names of particular historic events, documents, and periods.

   Examples:
   the American Revolution
   World War II
   the Declaration of Independence
   the Communist Manifesto
   the Renaissance
   the Middle Ages

4. Capitalize the names of particular brands or products.

   Examples:
   Skipslow Peanut Butter
   Snap 'n' Crackle Chewies

5. Capitalize the names of religions, races, nationalities, and languages.

   Examples:
   the Presbyterian Church
   the Roman Catholic Church
   Caucasian
   African-American
   French, English, Nigerian, Swahili, Urdu, Esperanto

6. Capitalize words that show a person's family relationship, rank, title, office, or profession when they are used with a person's name. Capitalize them if they are used as a name or form of address.

   Examples:
   Uncle Ezra, Cousin Molly
   Colonel Bush, Sergeant York
   Congressman Fernaldo, Senator Vastform, Governor Trask
   Superintendent Atkins

"Come here, Mother." ("Mother" is the name you are calling her, as distinguished from "My mother praised me.")

7. Capitalize the titles of important officeholders.

Examples:
the President of the United States
the Secretary of State

8. Capitalize geographical names such as those of states, nations, parks, lakes, oceans, cities, or streets.

Examples:
Massachusetts, Nevada
Ghana, the Soviet Union
Central Park, Fairmount Park
Lake Superior, Lake Baikal
the Pacific Ocean, the Mediterranean Sea
Chicago, Little Rock
Sesame Street, Swedesford Road

9. Capitalize the first, last, and all important words in titles. A *verb* in a title is always important, even if it is short—*Is, Am, See,* and the like.

Examples:
Zen and the Art of Motorcycle Maintenance
What Is the Purpose of Life?
Where in Heaven Are the Devils?
"Arnold Knocks the Dragon Down"
"The Night the Ghost Got In"
Mad
The New York Review of Books
the *Mona Lisa*

10. Capitalize words referring to God.

Example:
Praise God and give thanks to Him for His many

17

C

blessings. (But do not capitalize gods in general: All the gods of humankind are numerous and varied.)

11. In LETTERS, 84 capitalize the salutation and the first word of the complimentary close.

    Examples:
    Dear Sir:
    Dear Carlos,
    Very truly yours,
    Sincerely yours,

12. Capitalize the first word in each line of conventional POETRY, 114.

    Example:
    The downpour prickles on the pond, so sharp
    It hits the heads of shallow-floating carp.

    —SHIKI

    NOTE: Many modern poets do not follow this rule, using capitals only according to standard prose rules, or sometimes none at all.

13. Capitalize school subjects *only* when they are languages or the names of particular courses.

    Examples:
    Spanish
    Ancient African Civilizations
    Biology 2
    history
    biology

14. Capitalize the first word spoken in DIALOGUE, 51.

    Example:
    John said, "Please look away."

B. *When not to capitalize*
   In general, never capitalize unless you have a reason

to. The reason may be one of the rules above or because you wish to create a special effect.

1. Do *not* capitalize the names of animals, birds, flowers, trees, diseases, games, foods, and seasons unless they contain a PROPER NOUN, 123 (Tay-Sachs disease) or PROPER ADJECTIVE, 122 (English sparrow).

2. Do *not* capitalize such words as *senior class* or *upper school* unless they form a special name.

   Example:
   Junior High School Spring Dance

3. Do *not* capitalize NOUNS, 96 that follow a brand name unless they are a part of the name.

   Examples:
   Ford car, Kleenex tissue, Spearmint gum; but Toaster Tarts, the Volkswagen Rabbit

4. Do *not* capitalize points of the compass (east, south, north, west) except when referring to a region or a political entity.

   Examples:
   The East defeated the West in the play-off.
   The North won the Civil War.
   the Eastern bloc nations

5. Do *not* capitalize *a, an,* or *the* before a title or name unless they are a part of the title or name.

   Examples:
   the St. Louis *Post-Dispatch*; the *National Enquirer*; the Right Honorable Senator from Maine; *The Time Machine*; *Intruder in the Dust.*

6. Writers often have difficulty deciding whether or not to capitalize such words as *mother, father, uncle, aunt.* In general, do *not* capitalize them if they are not used as a name. (See A. 6 on page 3.)

C

Example:
My *m*other married my *f*ather in the presence of
two *a*unts and my old *g*randmother.

32. Cases

In English, NOUNS, 96 and PRONOUNS, 119 have three
cases (or forms): the SUBJECT, 153 case (often called the
subjective or the *nominative* case), the OBJECT, 98 case (or
objective case), and the *possessive* case. The case or form
of a noun or pronoun is determined by how the word is
used in a sentence.

Examples:

subject case	1. *I* groaned with pain.
	2. Afterward, *we* ate a gopher.
object case	1. The hero loved *her*.
	2. She didn't love *him*.
possessive case	*Joe's* toe is twisted. So is *mine*.
	Hers came completely off.

NOTE: An understanding of case is especially
useful in determining the form of *pronouns*. See
PRONOUNS, chart 119.

33. Clauses

A clause is a group of related words that contains a
SUBJECT, 153 and a VERB, 168.

Clauses can be classified in several ways; the following distinctions are of the most use to the writer of general material.

A. *Independent* or *main clause.*
This is the same as a SENTENCE, 139.

Example:

Molly	*was blowing*	bubble gum.
(subject)	(verb)	

B. *Dependent* or *subordinate clause.*
This is a clause that cannot stand alone; it needs the rest of the sentence to complete it.

Examples:
1. While Molly was blowing bubble gum,

      (subj.)   (verb)
    —— subordinate clause ——

there was a loud pop.
2. The girl who gave me a dirty look was

      (subj.)   (verb)
    —— subordinate clause ——

distressingly intelligent.

Two common types of the subordinate clauses are the *adjective clause* and the *adverb clause.*
An *adjective clause* modifies a noun in a sentence.

Examples:

1. Mrs. Jones, *who likes our dog,* rescued him from the dog catcher.

2. That historical novel, *which is long and complicated,* caught my interest.

3. Cars *that guzzle gas* impoverish drivers.

NOTES:
1. Generally the word *who* introduces adjective clauses that refer to people, the word *which* to things, and the word *that* to things or people or both.
2. For punctuation of adjective clauses within a sentence, see RESTRICTIVE CLAUSES, 131.

An *adverb clause* modifies a verb in a sentence.

Examples:

1. I *like* you *because you never scold me.*
   (verb)

2. *Although Bob likes me,* he *shouts* at my father.

Adverb clauses are introduced by a word called a *subordinator.* Some common subordinates are: *after, although, because, if, since, so that, unless, until, when, whenever,* and *while.* If you put a subordinator in front of a sentence, the result is a subordinate clause.

Example:
1. *Sentence* My house is my castle.
2. *Subordinate clause* unless my house is my castle . . .

The idea of the subordinate clause sounds as if it needs to be completed: "*Unless my house is my castle,* I'm going to move into your house."

> NOTE: When a subordinate clause begins a sentence, it is usually set off from the rest of the sentence by a comma (as in the example just above).

34. Clichés

A cliché is a trite, hackneyed expression that has been used so much that it has become weak and unconvincing.

Examples:
big as a house
a fluffy cloud
the silvery moon
keep the wolf from the door
grin and bear it
quick as lightning
slow as molasses in January

A cliché (a French word meaning, among other things, a rubber stamp) may have been effective the first few times it was used, but it has become stale. When writing, try for fresh ways of saying things.

35. Colons (:)

A colon calls the reader's attention to what comes next; it indicates that something is to follow.

Examples:
1. The results were very bad: nothing to eat for three days, four people down with pneumonia, and over $500 worth of lost equipment.
2. In life there are four things people can do with their hands: wring them in despair, fold them in apathy, put them in their pockets for safekeeping, or lay them on a job that needs doing.

The colon is also used:

1. to introduce a list (such as the following: flashlight, raincoat, rabbit's foot . . .)
2. after the salutation in a formal letter (Dear Sir: Gentlemen: Dear Ms. Pressler:)
3. in writing the time (6:25 P.M.)
4. in separating chapter and verse in Bible citations (Luke 3:7)

36. Commas (,)

The comma is used to separate items from each other, especially in sentences.

A. Use a comma to separate two SENTENCES, 139 joined by a coordinating CONJUNCTION (and, but, or, for), 41.

Example:
Francis thinks the food in the cafeteria is pure poison, *and* Jeffrey wants to know why they serve such small helpings.

> NOTE: If the two sentences are very short, no comma is required.
> *Example:*
> John smoked and Mary fumed.

B. The comma is never used when there is only one sentence with a single subject and a compound verb—

C

that is, where the *and* or *but* do not separate two complete sentences.

Example:

George   *saw*   himself in a mirror and *was* quite
(subject) (verb)   (verb)
upset.

C. The comma is used to set off APPOSITIVE PHRASES, C110.

Example:

My guest, *an old Chinese gentleman,* asked why football wasn't played by coolies.

D. The comma is generally used to set off introductory PHRASES, 110 or CLAUSES, 33 from the rest of the sentence.

Examples:

1. *Between the tree and bush,* a small crocus was growing. (phrase)
2. *After he had washed himself carefully,* Albert fell into the muck. (clause)
3. *Because the dog was awake,* he bit the thief. (clause)

E. Words in direct address are set off by commas.

Examples:

1. *John,* what do you think?
2. Oh, *God,* make the bad people good and the good people nice.
3. We saw you, *Frank,* at the game.

F. Commas are used to set off such words as *yes, no, well, however,* when they are used alone at the beginning of a sentence.

Examples:

1. *Yes,* I think so.
2. *However,* she did it poorly.
3. *Well,* let me think.

G. Set off interrupting expressions by commas.

Examples:
1. Little Boy Blue, *on the other hand,* did not lose his head.
2. It's better, *I suppose,* to lose your sheep.
3. These are, *as Tom Paine wrote in 1776,* the times that try men's souls.

H. Set off nonrestrictive clauses by commas, but not restrictive clauses. See RESTRICTIVE AND NONRESTRICTIVE CLAUSE, 131 for examples.
I. Use commas to separate items in a SERIES, 140.

Example:
Hooray for the red, white, and blue.

J. In DATES, 48 and ADDRESSES, 4, each item after the first one is set off by commas. See also LETTERS, 84.

37. Comparison of adjectives and adverbs

ADJECTIVES, 5 and most ADVERBS, 6 have three degrees of comparison: the positive, the comparative, and the superlative. The comparative compares two items, the superlative three or more.

Examples:

	positive degree	comparative degree	superlative degree
adjectives	big	bigger	biggest
	ugly	uglier	ugliest
	enormous	more enormous	most enormous
	terrible	more terrible	most terrible
adverbs	soon	sooner	soonest
	quietly	more quietly	most quietly
	interestingly	more interestingly	most interestingly

C

NOTES:
1. *Less* and *least* can be used instead of *more* and *most.*
   Example:
   The group was *less raucous* than yesterday and the *least attractive* of all the groups in town.
2. One- and two-syllable words are usually compared by adding *-er* or *-est* (happier, happiest).
3. Words of three or more syllables use *more* or *most* (most ridiculous—*not* ridiculousest).
4. When comparing two items, use the comparative degree.
   Example:
   The male twin was *healthier* than the female.
5. When comparing three or more items, use the superlative degree.
   Example:
   The last-born triplet was the *puniest.*

38. Complement, compliment

Be sure not to confuse the word *complement,* explained below, with *compliment,* pronounced the same way but with a totally different meaning: praise, approve, admire, as in: Oscar *complimented* Ralph on his new suit; Rosie paid her friend a *compliment.*

39. Complements

A *complement* is the word or expression that completes a statement and gives it meaning. Complements are often nouns and the object of the verb. Sometimes they are adjectives modifying the subject.

Examples:
1. He saw the *ocean.* (object of verb *saw*)
2. The ocean was *blue.* (modifies *ocean*)
3. It was the *Atlantic.* (modifies *it*)

See also NOUNS, 96 and VERBS, B168.

40. Compositions

For the purpose of this discussion, I define *composition* as an organized paper of moderate length dealing with a specific subject. It is not a SHORT STORY, 143, which is fiction, nor is it a REPORT, 130, which is primarily an organized presentation of information. *Essay* is another word with almost the same meaning as *composition*.

In writing a composition, never lose sight of the purpose of your paper. Why are you writing it, and for whom? Also consider the *material* you will use.

A. *Purpose*

Your *purpose* may be to entertain your readers, to give them information, to persuade them of some point of view (see PERSUASION, 109), to reassure them, to move them to action, or a combination of these. It will help to think about what you are trying to achieve before starting to figure out how to go about the writing.

B. *Material*

Your material may consist of opinions and information you already have in your head; don't overlook that source. Or it may be made up of notes you have taken on reading you have done (see NOTE-TAKING, 95), interviews or conversations you have had, or matters you have heard or seen on TV, on radio, or at the movies. Whatever the material, unless you have an amazingly well-organized and retentive mind, you will probably do a better job if you spend a little time arranging your material in some way before you start writing. Of course once you start to write, you will probably find that your arrangement needs some rearranging as you go. It is rarely possible simply to follow an OUTLINE, 102 in writing a full essay. Most writers find that the writing itself forces them to reshape the organization as they proceed. But having an outline or plan before they start helps avoid some pain and saves time later on.

C

C. Organization: beginning, middle, end

Most instruction on organizing a piece of writing tells students that their papers should have a beginning, a middle, and an end. It is obvious that you have to start a subject and you have to finish; what comes in between is the middle. But usually it is not as cut and dried as the old country preacher's formula for a good sermon—"First you tell 'em what you're going to tell 'em; then you tell 'em; then you tell 'em what you told 'em"—or as the King's directions to the White Rabbit in presenting evidence at the trial of the Knave in *Alice in Wonderland*: "Begin at the beginning, and go on till you come to the end: then stop." Still, you could do worse.

1. *Beginning* You do need to give some thought to the way to start your paper. Sometimes the beginning is the hardest part, and it may be better to try to write the middle first, deciding later on the best way to begin. One good way to begin a paper is with a *question*: "Why should students be required to attend classes when they are likely to learn more by staying out in the real world?" Or "What kind of knowledge of sex and love is a fifteen-year-old kid likely to pick up if he's never read a book on the subject?"

    Another way is to begin with a *statement*: "If you make your eyes really see and your ears really hear, you can figure out a lot about a neighborhood by just sitting for an hour on the front steps." Or "After talking with five teachers and ten students in my class, I believe there are three changes we ought to make at this school next year, and I intend to see that they are made."

    Don't turn your reader off by writing, "This is going to be a paper about . . ." or "I've been given the topic *fish* to write about, and . . ."

2. *Middle* You may want to start your essay right in the middle of the subject. In no case should you wait

28

too long to get to the real heart of the paper. The middle really constitutes the substance of what you have to say. It will be the longest part of the paper, the part that needs the most careful organizing and arranging.

A good way to organize ideas and information for an essay is to *list the main ideas,* following each with the points you might use to develop it: facts, examples, incidents, anecdotes, reasons, and explanations. If your subject is at all complicated, you will have to make such a listing in order to avoid getting confused.

While many people do not find it necessary, or even helpful, to follow a formal outline strictly, others do find such an outline useful (see OUTLINING, 102). If you do use an outline, think of it as a tool to serve you, not as a form that will dominate you.

3. *End* A good piece of writing ends in such a way that readers have a satisfying feeling that the work is finished. Of course they don't want to read some such phrasing as "And so I have shown that . . ." or "Now I bring my paper to a conclusion." But they do want to have a sense of completion. This ending can be another question arising from the material in the paper: "I've decided what I'm going to do about (whatever it is), but what are you going to do?" or "What have you seen in the past week that could prove me wrong?"

The ending can also consist of a vigorous restatement of the main idea of the paper: "It is true that in the real world out there we have crime, love, and action. We also have the vivid world of TV and the movies. But unless we can bring these realities into the schools, where through discussion and reading we can give some shape to them in our minds, we are more likely to end up confused than educated." Or "So it's not a matter of whether or not there will be sex education for fifteen-year-olds, but rather what kind of sex education there will be. Only the school with a free atmosphere, good teachers, and plenty of discussion is qualified to give the best kind."

D. *Paragraphing*

I feel that much of the instruction given under the heading "How to Write a Paragraph" is not very useful or realistic. It leads the student to suppose that real people organize their writing by thinking of topic sentences, by supporting the topic sentences with a few points, and by going on gracefully to the next topic sentence, supporting points, and so on, until the end. I don't know any professional writer who works that way.

And yet paragraphing is important. For one thing, the reader gets tired and discouraged looking at a page of writing or print that goes on and on with never a break. Readers need to be helped along by some signs of how the ideas in the paper are progressing. They want to be allowed to take a mental breath now and then before plunging back into the argument. Thus, you will make your readers happier and get your ideas across better if you write in PARAGRAPHS, 103.

The main points and subpoints in the outline or arrangement of ideas that you may have made before starting to write will probably, for the most part, turn out to be paragraphs in your paper (see also TRANSITIONS, 164). When you have finished the *first draft* of a paper (see REVISION OF PAPERS, 133), you will do well to look it over to check whether you have paragraphed it in a way that will be most helpful to your readers. In your first draft you can indicate that you want a new paragraph by using the sign ¶.

These suggestions should help in taking hold of any topic, idea, or assignment and coping with it adequately. As you become experienced in writing compositions, you will discover ways that especially suit your style. The suggestions will also help you organize your thinking and the information you have collected. No set of devices, however, can do your thinking or provide material for you.

For suggestions about how to do a first and final draft and on PROOFREADING, 121, see REVISION OF PAPERS, 133. For suggestions on a special kind of writing task, see REPORTS, 130; see also PERSUASION, 109.

The various steps I have explained involve what today is often called *process writing*—that is, the recognition that writing is a process: planning, prewriting, writing again, revising, proofreading, etc.

41. Conjunctions

A conjunction is one of the PARTS OF SPEECH, 107. It joins words or groups of words. The most common conjunctions are *and, but,* and *or;* they are called *coordinating conjunctions.* They join grammatically equal elements—words with words, PHRASES, 110 with phrases, SENTENCES, 139 with sentences.

> *Examples:*
> 1. good *or* bad (word with word)
> 2. in the store *but* out of sight (phrase with phrase)
> 3. We ate hot tamales, *and* they had cottage cheese. (sentence with sentence) See COMMAS, 36.

Another type of conjunction is the *subordinating conjunction.* See CLAUSES, 33; COMMAS, 36.

42. Context

Context refers to the words surrounding a word in a sentence or situation in which the word is used. The context of a word will often help to give you its meaning or tell you which of its several meanings the writer intends. For example, if you did not know the meaning of *enervated,* you could nevertheless understand it in the context of the sentence "After three days without food, he

C

was so enervated that he could not climb the last hill to reach camp."

Many words have several different meanings; the context indicates which one is intended. *Get,* for example, has over seventy meanings in English; some of them are clear from these sentences:

1. It really *gets* me when he giggles like that.
2. Please *get* some sleep tonight.
3. The bullet *got* him in the belly.
4. When she goes to a party, she *gets* intoxicated.

43. Contractions

A contraction is a shortened form of a word or number. An *apostrophe,* 18 is used to show where letters or numbers have been omitted.

Examples:
1. **don't** for *do not* (Don't do that.)
2. **it's** for *it is* (It's better now.)
3. **can't** for *cannot* (He can't juggle.)
4. **who's** for *who is* (Who's at the door?)
5. **'88** for *1988* (In '88 Bush was elected.)
6. **g'bye** for *goodbye*. (G'bye, all you kids.)

44. Conventions of English

ifyoufindthisparagraphhardtoreaditsbecauseithasab
solutelynopunctuationthatmeansnoeasywaytotellwhere
onewordendsandthenextwordbeginsnoeasywaytotellwhe
rethesentencesendandbeginnoeasywaytotellwhetherase
ntenceisaquestionorastatementitishardtogetsenseoutoft
helettersisntit

If you find this paragraph hard to read, it's because it has absolutely no punctuation. That means no easy way to tell where one word ends and the next word begins, no easy way to tell where the sentences end and begin, no easy way to tell whether a sentence is a question or a statement. It is hard to get sense out of the letters, isn't it?

---

naoweadmispelengtwothuhprobblumthamispelleen
izpurrfuktleelodgacculfrummafoanettikpoytavyoobuttd
uzzntuhgreawiththsistmyureyoostewthissmaykesitevun
horrdurtoogettthcencefrummthuwurdz

Now we add misspelling to the problem. The misspelling is perfectly logical from a phonetic point of view but doesn't agree with the system you're used to. This makes it even harder to get the sense from the words.

The paragraphs show that our language needs the *conventions* of

> word division,
> punctuation,
> capitalization, and
> spelling

to make it easier to extract the sense from the writing.

Learn the conventions of English—*these agreements among literate people about how to write our language*—for three reasons:

1. so that you can write more clearly and make yourself understood;
2. so that people who read what you write will not consider you ignorant; and
3. so that you can read accurately and easily the writing of others.

Once you have learned the conventions, you may want to break them on occasion, but you should break them only for good reasons, *knowing what you are doing* and to achieve some special effect, not out of ignorance.

The conventions of punctuation are given in this book under the names of the punctuation marks (commas, periods, question marks, and so on); the conventions for capitalization, dialogue (conversation), and spelling oc-

C

cur in the regular alphabetical listing. (See also STAN-DARD ENGLISH, 150.)

45. Copyright

If a book or other piece of writing is copyrighted—has a copyright—it means that no one is permitted to copy it without written permission. (The same is true for other kinds of creative work, such as music and movies.) The kinds of copying that are prohibited include photocopying, recording, and storing the material in a computer. The copyright is shown by the symbol ©, followed by a date or dates. (See also BOOKS, 27.)

46. Dangling modifiers

Dangling modifiers are MODIFIERS, 93, often PHRASES, 110, that do not clearly and sensibly modify a word in a sentence. Correctly used, most, but not all, modifying phrases immediately precede or follow the word they modify.

Examples:
1. *Wrong*
   Riding along with his eyes closed, a truck hit the boy. (The truck didn't have its eyes closed) (dangling participial phrase)
   Corrected
   Riding along with his eyes closed, the boy was hit by a truck.
2. *Wrong*
   Lying on the beach, the sun burned me badly. (dangling participial phrase)
   Corrected
   Lying on the beach, I was burned by the sun.
3. *Wrong*
   Although brief, I enjoyed our meeting. (dangling phrase)
   Corrected
   Although it was brief, I enjoyed our meeting.

See also PARTICIPLES, 106.

D

47. Dashes (—)

A dash is a longer line than a HYPHEN, 71. In typing, it is indicated by two hyphen marks: --

A. Dashes are used to indicate a major interruption of a sentence.

Examples:
1. All of us kids—the teacher always called us kids—decided to stay at home Tuesday.
2. Then the teacher—but you already know what she did.
3. Clark whispered, "Please get that thing away from—," but Francine stopped him by fainting.

B. Dashes are also used to show that some further explanation is coming.

Example:
Use dashes sparingly—only when you feel that nothing else will work as well.

NOTES:
1. Whether you use dashes, COMMAS, 36, or PARENTHESES, 105 to set off an interruption is a matter of taste. The interruption by dashes tends to be loud and strong, the interruption by parentheses to be more of a whispered aside, and the interruption by commas somewhere in between.
   Examples:
   1. *Gone With the Wind*—how I detested that old movie!—has at last left Cinema II.
   2. *Gone With the Wind* (my mother's favorite way to spend a few hours) has at last left Cinema II.
   3. *Gone With the Wind,* in case you hadn't heard, has at last left Cinema II.
2. Either a dash or a COLON, 35 can be used to indicate that something more is coming. In this case a dash is usually less strong and

definite than a colon—a kind of continuation
or afterthought.
Example:
A colon—well, see how it is used on page 23.

48. Dates

In writing dates, each item after the first one is set
off by commas (but there is no comma between the name
of the month and the number of the day.)

Examples:
1. Today is Wednesday, April 17, 1991.
2. On September 16, 1988, Flo expects to fly to the
   moon.

   EXCEPTION: No comma is used between the
   month and the year or after the year when the
   day is omitted.
   Example:
   They married in June 1930 and have been
   squabbling ever since.

49. Debating

A debate is a formal contest in argumentation between two individuals or teams, each taking opposite
sides of a well-defined question. It is different from a discussion in that the object of a debate is to win the argument, whereas the object of a discussion is to exchange
ideas on a subject. A debate is an exercise in PERSUASION,
109 through SPEECH-MAKING, 146, and the entries in this
book under those two headings will be useful to you as
you prepare for a debate.

The subject of a formal debate is stated as a *proposition,* thus:

"Resolved, that the system of grading at Elmquist
High School should be abolished and a pass/fail system
established"; or

"Resolved, that by law, anyone under twenty-five
years of age should be prohibited from smoking."

D

In setting up a debate it is important to choose a proposition that provokes an interesting and lively discussion. A good proposition should be debatable (that is, not obviously true or false), limited enough in scope so that the main elements of it can be dealt with in the length of time available, and appropriate to the knowledge and experience of the debaters and the audience. For example, the two propositions given above would probably work well for intelligent junior high, senior high, or college debaters, whereas propositions like "Resolved, that God exists"; or "Resolved, that motherhood is more important than fatherhood" are too vague, broad, and unprovable to be satisfactory.

In preparing for a debate, each side (made up of one, two, or three members) should first of all try to find all the issues on which there may be a clash of opinion and to list arguments, pro and con, probably in two columns. Once the issues are determined, each side assembles its arguments in as convincing a way as possible.

The side that defends the proposition is the *affirmative;* that which opposes the proposition is the *negative.* There are various ways a debate can be conducted. The most common is to have two speakers on each side and to program the speeches thus:

Principal speeches (five minutes each)
1. first affirmative
2. first negative
3. second affirmative
4. second negative

Rebuttal speeches (two minutes each)
1. first negative
2. first affirmative

The *principal* speeches are prepared in advance and present the main arguments. The *rebuttal* speeches are not prepared exactly in advance but give each side a chance to rebut—that is, to answer, disprove, and refute

38

the arguments of the other side. Sometimes a rebuttal speech may end in a brief summary or restatement of the side being defended.

The speeches are strictly timed; a speaker must stop at the end of his or her time, finished or not.

Since a debate is a contest, it is customary to have one or more judges listen to the speakers and then render a decision on which side has done the better job of presenting a convincing argument. The judges may be specialists in the subject being debated, members of the class or group before which the debate is taking place, or members of the faculty. The decision depends on the skills of persuasion demonstrated by each team, not on the basis of the affirmative or negative convictions of the judges.

One danger in debating is that each side may be so anxious to win that it distorts the truth or fails to become familiar with the arguments on both sides. To avoid this danger it is a good idea not to let each team know whether it will be defending the affirmative or negative side of the proposition until shortly before the debate starts, so that each team will be forced to become familiar with the evidence on both sides.

50. Diagraming sentences

Diagraming is a method for showing with horizontal, vertical, and slanting lines how the various parts of a sentence relate to each other.

Examples:

1. The sentence *The small wooden bridge over the creek suddenly snapped.* would be diagramed thus:

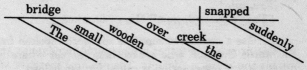

D

2. The sentence *Small children greatly love new toys, and they also love their parents.* would be diagramed thus:

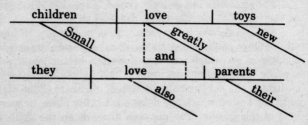

Some students enjoy sentence diagraming, and the practice may help their writing style. More often, however, the activity does not lead to much improvement in people's writing or reading ability. The time is probably better spent in writing and discussing and then revising the writing. Nevertheless, if you want to learn to diagram sentences, you will find the method further explained in many traditional grammar books.

51. Dialogue

A good way to make SHORT STORIES, 143 and other narrative writing interesting and to reveal the personalities of the characters is to write dialogue—that is, to set down the words the characters speak. There are specific rules for the punctuation and capitalization of dialogue.

1. Enclose in quotation marks the words actually spoken.

Example:
"That's an explosion," Mary remarked.

2. Use a comma to separate the words spoken from the words that tell who spoke them (except where another form of punctuation is called for; see below).

Examples:
1. "Well, keep calm," George said.
2. Oscar shouted, "Why should I?"

3. Capitalize the first word spoken.

Example:
Mary whispered, "We're all trying to be calm."

4. If the spoken words are an exclamation or a question, use an exclamation point or a question mark at the end of the quoted words instead of a comma.

Examples:
1. "Be quiet, you wretch!" the man shouted.
2. "Why do we have to be quiet?" asked Molly.

5. If a sentence of dialogue is divided into two parts by such words as *he said* or *she complained,* the second part of the quotation begins with a lower case letter because it is still the same sentence.

Example:
"Doing exercises," said Anna, "is my favorite form of torture."

6. If the second part of the quotation is a new sentence, it begins with a capital letter, and the quotation mark is preceded by a period.

Example:
"I'm not educating myself to earn a living," Abraham Lincoln said. "No, I'm trying to learn what to do with a living if I ever earn it."

7. If more than one sentence is spoken, do not close the quote until the speaker has finished.

Example:
When asked if he had ever been kicked by a certain mule, the driver replied, "No, sir, he's never kicked me yet. However, sir, he frequently kicks the place where I recently was."

D

8. Generally, the quotation marks *follow* any other punctuation.

Examples:
1. "Look at my dress," Mary said.
2. His grandmother snarled, "You go wash out your mouth with soap."
3. He constantly used the expression "uglification."

NOTE: Cases in which a statement is quoted within a question are an exception.
Example:
Did Maud actually say, "I refuse to punctuate"?

9. Use single quotation marks to indicate a quotation within a quotation.

Example:
Mr. Jackson explained, "It was Patrick Henry who said, 'Give me liberty or give me death!' "

10. In writing dialogue (conversation), begin a new paragraph whenever the speaker changes, even if only one word is spoken. But be sure that the quotation and such phrases as "he said" are in the same paragraph. Consult stories and novels and pages 149–151 of this book to see how it is handled in professional writing.

11. In real life people often speak in incomplete sentences. This informality may be reflected in written dialogue.

Example:
"Where did you get that crazy hat?" asked Zack.
"From the gutter," Solomon replied.
"From the gutter?" asked Zack.
"Yes, Zack, from the gutter, the good old friendly gutter where I also got my socks," Solomon said.

12. People also tend to interrupt each other in conversations. Interruptions are indicated by a DASH: —.

Example:

"You say you got your socks from—" Zack started to ask.

"Yes, that's what I said," Solomon shouted.

NOTES:
1. Do not use quotation marks to enclose an *in-direct* quotation—that is, when you are not quoting a person's words directly.
   Examples:
   indirect   H. L. Mencken wrote that Puritan-ism is the lurking fear that some-one somewhere is happy.
   direct   H. L. Mencken wrote, "Puritanism is the lurking fear that someone somewhere is happy."
2. Dialogue is also a major part of writing PLAYS, 112.

52. Dictionaries

Every household should contain a good, recently published dictionary. There are inexpensive paperback dictionaries, which can easily be carried back and forth to school; at home, a so-called college or collegiate abridged dictionary, containing about 150,000 defini-tions, is most useful. For people with a particular inter-est in language, an unabridged dictionary, containing from 250,000 to 500,000 definitions, can be helpful.

Each dictionary gives complete instructions for its own use and has a table of contents to show what the book contains in addition to the main section (appendices listing common abbreviations, sections on grammatical rules, and the like).

Here are some facts about the content and organi-zation of dictionaries.

A. *Alphabetical order*

The words defined in the dictionary always appear in alphabetical order: *pouch, poultice, poultry, pounce,*

D

pound, pour. Note that you have to read to the fourth or fifth letter to find each of these words, since they all begin with *pou-,* two begin with *poul-,* and two with *poun-.* (See ALPHABET, 12.)

B. *Guide words*

At the top of each page of a dictionary, printed in heavy type, are *guide words.* The first of these is the first word on the page, and the second is the last. All the other words on the page come alphabetically between the guide words.

C. *Definitions*

Dictionaries list all the major definitions of a word. Many of them do so *chronologically*—that is, they give the *earliest* meaning attributed to a word first. Others arrange meanings by *frequency*—that is, the most *common* meaning is given first. The dictionary's preface generally tells which practice has been followed. In order to find the correct definition you are looking for, you must have some idea of the CONTEXT, 42 in which the word is employed. For example, the word *fair* can mean beautiful (a *fair* maiden); clean, spotless, without error (a *fair* copy); light in color, blond (*fair* skin); clear (*fair* weather); just and honest (a *fair* price; *fair* play); and so on.

D. *Parts of speech*

Many words can be used as different PARTS OF SPEECH, 107. To get the meaning you want, consult the part-of-speech labels in the dictionary: *n.* = noun; *pron.* = pronoun; *v.* (or *v.i.* and *v.t.*) = verb; *adj.* = adjective; *adv.* = adverb; *prep.* = preposition; *conj.* = conjunction; and *interj.* = interjection.

Example:
open, *adj.* 1. not closed. 2. spread out. 3. available. *v.* 1. to make open. 2. to spread out. 3. to start operating.

For major words and in the case of words that are
spelled the same but have two distinct meanings (as *bear,*
the animal, and *bear,* the verb meaning "support, carry"),
two separate entries are generally used.

E. *Pronunciation*

The dictionary gives the pronunciation of words,
usually in parentheses after the main entry: **op·pose**
(ə pōz´). The accent mark ´ shows that the accent is on
the syllable *pose;* the line over the *o* is called a *macron*
(mā´kron) and means that the *o* is sounded long—is pronounced like itself. Another very common mark of pronunciation is the *schwa* (ə) (see *oppose* above). It
represents an unaccented sound "uh," as *a* in *ago, e* in
agent, or *i* in *pencil.* These pronunciation indicators are
called *diacritical marks.* Most dictionaries give a key to
pronunciation at the bottom of every other page.

F. *Usage*

Most dictionaries precede the definition of some
words by a word or phrase to indicate that the word is
used only under special circumstances. Some terms or
spellings, for example, are common in Great Britain but
not in the United States; for those, the dictionary will
note "chiefly Brit." or "Brit."

> *Example:*
> **pet·rol** . . . *n* . . . *Brit:* gasoline.

Other such labels may include *arch.* (archaic—that is, old-
fashioned and now rarely used), *obsolete* (no longer used,
out of date), *slang, var.* (variant), *obsc.* (obscene), *subst.*
(substandard), and *dial.* (dialect, usually with a geographical designation, as *dial. New England*).

G. *Spelling*

The dictionary shows how to spell a word and sometimes gives alternative spellings.

Example:
judgment (sometimes also *judgement*).

It also shows how to divide the word into syllables, information that you need when breaking a word at the end of a line.

Example:
op•po•si•tion

H. *Word derivation*

Either preceding or following the definitions of a word, most dictionaries include a note on the word's etymology—its derivation from other languages or earlier forms of the English language. These word derivations are generally enclosed in brackets ([]) and use an arrow or the symbol + to show sequence. Abbreviations for other languages are generally explained in the preface.

> NOTE: Knowing the derivation of a word may help to clarify a word's current meaning by showing how it has been used in past times and other places, but it will seldom tell exactly what it means today.

I. *Synonyms and antonyms*

Larger dictionaries often follow the definition of common words by a discussion of their *synonyms* (words having nearly the same meaning) and *antonyms* (words having the opposite meaning).

Example:
prejudice ... Syn. (noun) bias, partiality.

For a more complete set of synonyms, refer to a THESAURUS, 162.

Because different dictionaries use different styles and systems, it is essential to read the explanations at the front of the particular work to understand its organization and symbols.

53. Direct objects

The direct object is a word in a sentence that receives the action of a verb.

Examples:

1. George hit the *tree*.
   (verb)   *(direct object)*

2. *Mary* flattered *him*.
   (verb)   (direct object)

3. Please take those ugly *pictures* down.
   (verb)   (direct object)

54. Discussions

One of the best ways to achieve competence in English (and in any other language, and in life) is to discuss important, interesting questions. Discussion stimulates your mind, teaches you to think, and challenges you to express yourself well. It does this whether you are in class, in a group out of school, or just with one or two other people.

A true discussion is an exchange of ideas on an interesting subject. It is *not* a recitation (where the teacher asks you to tell the right answer) or an argument or a DEBATE, 49 (where you are trying to win). Further, the subject of a discussion should not be a simple question with a factual answer: Does 2 + 2 = 4? What is Eli's address? How many states are there in the U.S.A.? There are thousands of good questions for discussion *Examples:* (or discussion topics). Is it ever okay to tell a lie? What causes some people to cheat? What are some good ways to encourage people? Why did (whoever) do (whatever) in the story we just read? Would students learn more if summer vacation were shortened to one month?

In a class or a group, sometimes it is useful to ask, "Could we discuss that point Kevin just made?" or "I'd

like to challenge that statement—may I?" Don't be afraid
to take the initiative *and* don't be afraid to put forward
for discussion an idea that may turn out to be wrong.
You're trying to learn, not to win.

Be sure that you don't insist on discussion if it turns
out that it will be interrupting something important that
needs to be done right now, or if the discussion might
seriously embarrass someone. A couple of other points: It
usually helps to make the discussion work better in
school if you raise your hand and wait to be called on
rather than just blurting out an opinion. Also, don't be
afraid if, after a good question is raised, there is a period
of thinking and several hands are raised before any person is called upon. "Wait time" thinking about a good
questions is very educational and helps develop competence.

Discussion writing: When you are assigned a paper
to discuss a topic, think about the topic carefully; note
down various points and points of view to express; try to
look at the topic from all sides; perhaps discuss it orally
with your friends or family before you start to write; organize your thoughts in a rough OUTLINE, 102; and try to
come to a conclusion about the topic, even if the conclusion is not a statement but, rather, two or three questions that you believe people should think about. (See
also COMPOSITIONS, 40.)

55. Disinterested, uninterested See UNINTER-
ESTED, 167.

56. Double negatives

A double negative is a construction, a sentence, or
other expression, that says *no* or *not* twice.

Examples
1. I can*'t hardly* hear you.
   (Correct: I can hardly hear you.)

2. She did*n't* have *no* idea.
   (Correct: She had no idea.
   She didn't have any idea.)

Even though the meaning of the statement is usually clear, the English is NONSTANDARD, 94—it often sounds ignorant, especially in writing.

E

57. etc.

The abbreviation "etc." (from the Latin *et cetera,* "and others") should not be used in any writing more formal than a personal letter. The expressions "and so on" or "and the like" are preferable, but usually it makes for stronger writing to add one or two more examples and omit "and so on."

Example:
"A healthful diet includes green vegetables—beans, peas, broccoli, and the like."

Never write "and etc.," and never use "etc." after just one item.

58. Exclamation points (!)

An exclamation point indicates the end of an exclamation—a statement or utterance expressing strong emphasis or emotion. Sentences that end in an exclamation point are called *exclamatory sentences.*

Examples:
1. Come here this instant! (emphasis)
2. The dogs are attacking the rabbits again! (emotion)
3. Hurray! Wow! Heavens! Help! (emotion)

   NOTES:
   1. Use an exclamation point in sentences that are not questions but begin with *what, why,* or *how.*

50

Examples:
1. What a fine day!
2. How bored I am!

2. Never use more than one exclamation point unless you are writing comic strips. In general, use the exclamation point sparingly. If in doubt, leave it out.

59. Fact and opinion

To write or speak well and honestly, you must know the difference between facts and opinions. A fact is a statement that can be proven true. (*Example:* March has thirty-one days.) An opinion may be based on a fact or some facts but it is a view or a belief held by a person. (*Example:* March is the best month of the year.) You should check your "facts" to make sure they are true. If you write an opinion, don't try to pass it off as a fact. That is dishonest.

Also, to be an intelligent reader, you should be careful as you are reading to figure out whether the author is writing facts or opinions. If you aren't careful, you may be led astray.

60. Farther, further

Use *farther* when you refer to a physical distance ("farther away"). Use *further* when you mean more or additional ("further evidence").

Examples:
1. She carried the load two miles farther but then set it down and made no further effort.
2. The further he thought about it, the greener the grass seemed in the farther field.

61. Figurative language

Figurative language in speech and writing involves using comparisons—figures of speech. The two most common figures of speech are *metaphors* and *similes*. The opposite of figurative language is literal language.

Examples:

1. *literal*   The eagle holds on to the crag with his claws, high up in the lonely blue spaces of air on a sunny day.

   figurative   "He clasps the crag with crooked hands,
Close to the sun in azure lands."
—ALFRED TENNYSON

2. *literal*   His dreams were small, pleasant, and disorganized.

   figurative   "His dreams were light as feathers, and blew this way and that."
—JOHN UPDIKE

In the first example the eagle doesn't literally have crooked hands, but that is what they remind Tennyson of; nor are the great spaces of blue sky "azure lands," but calling them that strikes the reader. The user of figurative language sees one thing in terms of another; he or she employs an enlightening, impressive sort of double vision. In the second example, Updike sees dreams as feathers and their lack of organization as a random drift.

Two commonly distinguished figures of speech are *similes* and *metaphors*.

A. **Similes**

A simile expresses comparison using *like* or *as*.

Examples:

1. "The pigeons are *pompous as bankers.*"
—PHYLLIS MCGINLEY
2. "Ali drove a right *straight as a pole* into the stunned center of Foreman's head."
—NORMAN MAILER
3. "Dawn comes up *like thunder* out of China 'crost the bay!" —RUDYARD KIPLING

F

4. "The exhausted light [from the fireplace] beat up and down the wall . . . *like a bird trying to find its way out of the room.*" —EUDORA WELTY
5. "His rosy hands were folded on the shiny desk, reflected *like water flowers.*" —JOHN UPDIKE

B. *Metaphors*

A metaphor expresses comparison without the use of *like* or *as.*

Examples:
1. "Wind is a cat that prowls the night."
   —ETHEL ROMIG FULLER
2. "Life's but a walking shadow . . . , a tale told by an idiot . . ." —WILLIAM SHAKESPEARE
3. "Suddenly Ali hit him again. . . . The sound of a bat thunking into a watermelon was heard around the ring." —NORMAN MAILER
4. Lincoln's "thoughts were roots that firmly grasped the granite truth." —EDWIN MARKHAM
5. "Hunger is the best of cooks."
   —GERMAN PROVERB

In writing, use similes and metaphors not as ornaments but as ways to make your readers see and feel what you want them to or to express the way you see and feel.

Be careful not to use *mixed metaphors,* in which the comparison changes form, unless you are trying to be funny.

Examples:
1. When we first met, he bristled like a porcupine, but as we talked he began to thaw. (The comparison changes from porcupine to ice.)
2. He's a big wheel on the student council, but he doesn't know which end is up. (Wheels don't have ends, nor do they think about them.)

54

3. She's the mainspring of the speech team and really bowls them over in a debate. (The comparison
changes from a spring to a bowling ball.)
4. The American eagle will never turn tail and run.
(An eagle doesn't run or turn tail like a rabbit or
deer.)

When you read, try to recognize when the writer is
using figurative language. Otherwise, you may miss
much of the meaning. The poet Robert Frost said, "Poetry is a way of saying something while saying something else." (See POETRY, 114.)

C. *Other common figures of speech*

Apostrophe An apostrophe is a figure of speech in which
the writer or speaker directly addresses an object that
cannot understand, as in Edna St. Vincent Millay's poem
"God's World":
   "O World, I cannot hold thee close enough!"

> NOTE: *Apostrophe* the figure of speech is en-
> tirely different from APOSTROPHE the punctua-
> tion mark.

Hyperbole Hyperbole is exaggeration for special effect,
as when Shakespeare's Lady Macbeth looks at her hand
that helped Macbeth murder King Duncan and says, "All
the perfumes of Arabia will not sweeten this little
hand."

Irony To use irony is to say something but mean the
opposite, usually in a bitter or humorous manner, as
when a coach says to the outfielder who just dropped an
easy fly, "That was a great play," or the British soldier-
poet Siegfried Sassoon writes:

   "Does it matter?—losing your sight? . . .
   There's such splendid work for the blind."

55

F

Personification Personification is treating an inanimate thing or idea as if it were a person, or treating oneself as an inanimate object or idea.

Examples:
1. The floods clap their hands. —JOHN MILTON
2. I am a copper wire slung in the air,
   Slim against the sun I make not even a clear line of shadow. —CARL SANDBURG

62. Footnotes

When you cite a source in writing a formal paper, either quoting the expert's exact words or giving a summary of the author's ideas, identify the source by a *footnote* at the bottom of the page. Each footnote in the paper should be numbered in sequence, starting with the number 1. Place the number, raised a little above the line, at the end of the quotation or reference in the text; place the same number in front of the footnote that appears at the end of the page.

The purpose of footnotes is to tell your readers exactly where your information comes from in case they want to check or to read more, and also to give them an indication of how reliable your paper is.

There are a number of styles for writing footnotes; I give the most commonly used one here. Major items of information in a footnote are separated by commas, and the footnote should contain: (1) the author's name, first name or initials first; (2) the title of the work cited—use quotation marks for an article or chapter title; underline (italicize) the name of a magazine or title of a book; (3) for books, the place of publication and the name of the publisher in parentheses; (4) the number of the volume (if there are two or more); (5) date of the publication; and (6) page number(s).

Examples:

book	Isser Harel, *The House on Garibaldi Street,* New York (The Viking Press), 1975, pp. 73–76.
magazine	Isaac Asimov, "Clippings from Tomorrow's Newspapers, News Stories of 2024," *Saturday Review,* August 24, 1974, pp. 78–81.[1]

Footnotes may also be used to give additional information or explanation that might interrupt the text. Note the examples used at the bottom of this page. If there are only a few footnotes and not more than one per page, you may use an ASTERISK, 22 (*) instead of a number.

If you use the same reference more than once, abbreviate the reference after the first full citation:

Examples:
1. If citing the title in the footnote directly before, either, "Harel, pp. 92–93" or, "*ibid.,*[2] pp. 92–93."
2. If citing a title referred to again after other footnotes have intervened, either, "Asimov, *op. cit.,*[3] p. 82" or, "Asimov, p. 82."

NOTES:
1. Some teachers and publishers insist on a particular style in footnotes. Since there are several acceptable ways, be sure you find out exactly what style is expected before you work up your final draft.
2. While footnotes may make your paper look scholarly, they can also render it ponderous

---

[1] Note that the most common form used in a footnote is slightly different from that used in listing a source in a BIBLIOGRAPHY, 23.

[2] *ibid.,* from the Latin *ibidem,* meaning "in the same place."

[3] *op. cit.,* from the Latin *operea citato,* meaning "in the work cited."

---

and harder to read. Use footnotes sparingly, especially if you are not preparing a scholarly report.

63. Form for papers

Whenever you work on a paper as an assignment for a teacher, be sure you know what form the teacher wishes you to use. You may feel that the teacher is excessively fussy to insist on a particular form. In fact, the teacher's job of reading and commenting on a mass of papers is made easier if they all are in the same form, and it's no more work for you. If no form is prescribed, a convenient one is the following:

	Name Date Grade & Section
← 1½″ → (margin to allow for comments and corrections)	Title or Label
	(skip a line)
	This is the beginning of the

64. Frame tests (part of speech test)

A frame test is a sentence made up especially for the purpose of testing out to what PART OF SPEECH, 107 words belong. It has a blank in it in which only one part of speech will fit sensibly. If you need to know whether a word can be used as a noun, verb, linking verb, adjective, adverb, or preposition, try it out in the frame tests. Frame tests do not always work, but they are often helpful in giving you a sense of the function of words. The most useful frame tests follow.

Noun: I am happy about (the) _____.
(noun)

Verb: Let's _____ (it).
(verb)

    (Such endings of verbs as *-ing* or *-ed* must be removed to make the frame test work.)

Linking verb: They _____ nice.

(linking verb)

Adjective: The thing was very _____.

(adjective)

(The endings *-er* or *-est* must be removed from the adjective to make the frame test work.)

Adverb: Either: He said it _____ or: He _____

(adverb) (adverb)
said it.

Preposition: It went _____the thing(s).

(preposition)

(This frame test will not work for the very common preposition *of.*)

G

65. Gerund phrases

A gerund phrase is a phrase containing a GERUND, 66. A gerund phrase is used as a NOUN, 96.

Examples:
1. *His habitual snoring* slowly drove me wild.
2. After a vacation, I hate *arriving at home.*
3. Beneath *the roaring of traffic,* men were silently conspiring.

66. Gerunds

A gerund is a form of a VERB, 168 used like a NOUN, 96. Like a noun, it can be used as SUBJECT, 153; COMPLEMENT, 39; or OBJECT, 98.

Examples:
1. *Giggling* is a form of nervousness. (subject)
2. His worst habit is loud *giggling.* (complement)
3. Mr. Jacob's frankness stopped our *giggling.* (direct object)
4. She fell asleep during the *giggling.* (object of preposition)

NOTE: Gerunds end in *-ing.* They are not to be confused with PARTICIPLES, 105, many of which also end in *-ing,* but are used as adjectives.

67. Glossary

The glossary is a list of definitions or explanations of technical, special, or foreign words. It is usually placed near the end of a book.

68. Grammar

English grammar is the way our language puts words together into sentences to make sense. "My grandmother nice old that dog little bothers" is not a grammatical English sentence. But when the same eight words are put in grammatical order, we get a good sentence: "My nice old grandmother bothers that little dog." The same words in a different order make another good sentence with an entirely different meaning: "My little dog bothers that nice old grandmother." Thus you can see that *word order* is a very important principle of English grammar.

Another principle is *position.* "Grandmother bothers dog" means something quite different from "Dog bothers grandmother." SUBJECT, 153; VERB, 168; OBJECT, 98 is the most common order of words in English sentences, with other words, MODIFIERS, 93, put in to increase and clarify meaning.

Another way to see the importance of position of words in English grammar is to observe what happens when the ADVERB, 6 *only* is put in different places:

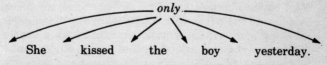

Read aloud the six positions of *only* and notice the drastic changes in meaning.

Another principle of grammar, less important in English than in many other languages, is *inflection*— changes in the *endings* of words and in their *form.* The most important inflectional changes in modern English

G

are endings, mainly *s* and *es* to show plurals in NOUNS, 96; *'s* and *s'* to show possession (see APOSTROPHES, 18) in nouns; *ed, en, s,* and *ing* to show changes in TENSE, 160 in VERBS, 168; and *ly, er,* and *est* to show COMPARISON, 37 in adverbs and adjectives. PRONOUNS, 119, however, change form rather than ending: *he, his, him; she, hers, her; I, mine, my, me;* and so on (as in "*He* gives it to *me*" compared to "*I* give it to *him.*" *He* and *I* are the subjective form; *him* and *me* are the objective form. There are some languages, like Latin, in which the changing endings and forms of words are even more important than the order of words. Thus Latin is a highly inflected language; English is not.

Another part of grammar is called *usage*—the study of what is correct and incorrect, acceptable and unacceptable. A sentence such as "He don't allow nobody do nothing where he live at" makes its meaning perfectly clear. But the usage is not acceptable as STANDARD ENGLISH, 150. It is NONSTANDARD, 94. For many people, speaking standard, "correct" English is important, and people who deviate from standard usage (except on purpose for special reasons) risk being thought ignorant, crude, or uneducated, even though they may be none of these. In a situation where you want to avoid giving such an impression, it is helpful to use standard English. It helps to get along and up in the mainstream world.

Is it useful to study grammar formally in school? Most educated people believe it is, but there's not much evidence to show that such study, all by itself, improves speaking and writing. It does, however, teach a usable vocabulary of terms and ideas that enable students and teachers to confer efficiently about writing and thus, one hopes, to improve it. The best way to use the many grammar entries in this book is for review purposes and reference. However, you can also learn grammar from the book by reading the main entries somewhat in this order: SENTENCES, 139; PARTS OF SPEECH, 107 (NOUNS, 96; PRONOUNS, 119; VERBS, 168; ADJECTIVES, 5; ADVERBS, 6; PREPO-

SITIONS, 116; CONJUNCTIONS, 41; and INTERJECTIONS, 79);
FRAME TESTS, 64 (a rather neat way of telling what part
of speech a word may be); CLAUSES, 33; PHRASES, 110; SUB-
JECTS, 153; OBJECTS, 98; TENSES, 160. Be sure to keep applying what you learn to your writing and speaking.

Grammar is a complex subject. Try to make certain
that studying it helps you to write and speak as you want
and need to. Don't let it make you so afraid of making a
mistake that you hardly dare write or speak at all in
school, on the job, or in company.

H

69. Homework   See STUDY SKILLS, 152.

70. Homonyms
Homonyms are words that have the same pronunciation but different spellings and different meanings.

Examples:
meat, meet; hear, here; their, there, they're; clause, claws.

71. Hyphens (-)
A hyphen is used either to show where words are divided or to indicate the joining of two closely related words (like fund-raising, self-seeker).

A. Use a hyphen to divide a word at the end of a line, between syllables (see SYLLABICATION, 155). If you do not know where to make the division, refer to a DICTIONARY, 52. *Never* divide a one-syllable word.

Examples:
1. Please do not inter-
   rupt while I sing.
2. The little child was crying buckets of tears.

> NOTE: Generally, words are divided after a PREFIX, 115 (sub-
> conscious),

before a SUFFIX, 154 (cumber-
some),
and between double letters (cin-
namon).

B. Use a hyphen when writing out numbers under one
hundred.

Examples:
twenty-five; ninety-nine

C. Use a hyphen to join two words that together modify
a NOUN, 96 (see MODIFIERS, 93).

Examples:
1. a two-thirds majority
2. a self-sealing bottle
3. the pine-forested hill

D. Always use a hyphen with such prefixes as *self-, ex-,*
and *all-.*

Examples:
self-employed, ex-president, all-American

72. Idioms

An idiom is a word, phrase, or expression that means something different from what is actually said or written.

Examples:
1. Bob was *in over his head* means: Bob couldn't understand or deal with the situation.
2. She's a *snake in the grass* means: She can't be trusted.

73. i.e.

From the Latin *id est,* meaning "that is."

Example:
She was omnivorous (*i.e.,* could eat anything).

74. Imply, infer

Imply and infer are two words whose meanings are often confused. *Imply* means to suggest something without actually saying it.

Examples:
1. He implied that he was very rich.
2. "What do you imply by that?" her mother asked.

Infer means to get or gather a certain meaning from a comment or action.

Examples:
1. Because he drove a Cadillac, I inferred that he was rich.
2. "When you roll your eyes like that, I infer that you don't like my suggestion," said the teacher.

75. Indirect objects

The indirect object is a NOUN, 96 or PRONOUN, 119 in a sentence that tells to *whom* or *what*, or for *whom* or *what*, the action of the VERB, 168 is done.

Examples:
1. Lolly gave the *kid*   a black eye. (to whom)
        (ind. obj.)
2. Thus she earned the *school* a bad reputation.
              (ind. obj.)
  (for what)
3. Buy *me*   a lollipop, Mom. (for whom)
    (ind. obj.)

NOTES:
1. When the words *to* or *for* are used, the words following them are parts of prepositional phrases, rather than indirect objects.
Examples:
prepositional phrases. The crowds gave a great ovation *to Lindbergh.*
Mother cooked some stew *for the family.*
indirect objects. The crowds gave *Lindbergh* a great ovation.
Mother cooked the *family* some stew.
2. The indirect object precedes the *direct object.*
3. When you use a pronoun as an indirect object, use its objective form *me, him, her, them,* and so on.
See also DIRECT OBJECTS, 53.

76. Indirect quotations

An indirect quotation reports what someone said without reproducing the exact words.

Examples:
1. Direct quotation: Elise screamed, "Let me go!"
2. Indirect quotation: Elise screamed that she wanted to be let go.
3. Direct quotation: Gabe grumbled, "Drop dead."
4. Indirect quotation: Gabe grumbled that we should drop dead.

77. Infinitive phrases

An infinitive phrase is a PHRASE, 110 containing an INFINITIVE, 78. The infinitive phrase may be used different ways in a sentence.

Examples:
1. *To refuse to talk with your parents* may cause them to start prying. (as noun)
2. He was delighted *to hide in the woods.* (as adverb)
3. The whole class ran out *to observe the scene.* (as adverb)

78. Infinitives

The infinitive is a verb form with the word *to* before it: "to exaggerate"; "to slather"; "to prove"; "to annoy"; "to trample."

Infinitives can be used as NOUNS, 96; ADJECTIVES, 5; or ADVERBS, 6.

Examples:
1. *To laugh* is less creative than *to weep.* (as nouns—subject and complement)
2. The bear decided *to wait* behind the rock. (as noun, object of verb)
3. Meals *to eat* and clothes *to wear* are better than daffodils *to contemplate.* (as adjectives, modifying nouns)
4. Henry's sister hit him *to make* him angry. (as adverb, modifying verb)

79. Interjections

An interjection is one of the eight PARTS OF SPEECH, 107 in traditional GRAMMAR, 68. It is a word that has little grammatical relation to other words in a sentence, and it often expresses emotion: "Wow!" "Heavens!" "Goodness!" "Whew!"

> *Examples:*
> 1. *My,* you look wretched today!
> 2. *Ouch!* You got me where it hurts!
> 2. *Well,* let's get started.

80. Interviewing

A good way to get information for COMPOSITIONS, 40 and REPORTS, 130 is to interview people who are experts on your topic or whose opinions may be interesting. Interviews are also a good way to get a sampling of people's opinions on various questions. Here are some suggestions that will help you make the most of a planned interview:

A. If the person to be interviewed (the interviewee) is often busy, make an appointment in advance.

B. Prepare your questions before the interview so that you can make best use of your time. In preparing, think about the topic and about what the interviewee is likely to know.

C. Use your questions, but don't insist upon sticking to them or proceeding in the order you have listed them. Often the interviewee will have important information that never occurred to you, or one question may suggest another very useful one. Sometimes a very good question is: What are the most important things you think I should know about this topic? Another is: Have we omitted any important things I should know about?

D. However, do try to keep the interviewee on the subject. If he or she gets off the topic, ask a question to bring the interview back on track.

E. If you don't understand something the inter-

viewee has said, say so politely and ask him or her to
clarify it or to explain again or to give an example.

F. Take notes (see NOTE-TAKING, especially D95). If
the interviewee goes too fast for you, ask him or her to
stop for a moment, especially if the point is important. A
tape recorder lets you avoid this problem. However, be
sure the interviewee agrees to be taped.

G. As soon as possible after the interview, read over
your notes. They may need clarifying while the topic is
still fresh in your mind.

H. Be sure you note down the exact position and title
(if any) of the interviewee, and give this information, perhaps in a FOOTNOTE, 62, if the interview is a part of a
report you are writing.

81. Irregular verbs

An irregular VERB, 168 is one that does not form its
past or present participle in the regular way.

The regular form is:

present	*past*	*past participle*
enjoy	enjoyed	(have) enjoyed
imagine	imagined	(have) imagined

The following are a few common irregular verbs:

present	*past*	*past participle*
think	thought	(have) thought
speak	spoke	(have) spoken
know	knew	(have) known
am, are	was, were	(have) been
fall	fell	(have) fallen

If you are not sure how an irregular verb forms its
PRINCIPAL PARTS, 117, check the dictionary. Irregular
forms will be listed, usually immediately following the
entry word and before the definitions.

NOTES:
1. These verbs cause much trouble in English, especially for people who do not have a good ear for language or whose native language is not English.
2. Most long verbs and all verbs that are relatively new to English (such as *rocket, contact,* and *brainstorm*) are regular. Little children just learning to speak, with good grammatical logic, often make mistakes by using irregular verbs as if they were regular: "I speak; I speaked yesterday; Mama thinks? Mama thinked; she has thinked all day."

82. Italics

Italics are letters that lean to the right *like this.* In typing or handwriting, they are indicated by underlining. Italics are used to emphasize a word or words or to indicate that you are writing about a word.

Examples:
1. Please arrive *exactly* on time. (emphasis)
2. He used *cuckoo* three times in the first paragraph. (indicating word written about)

83. Language

Human language is a system of symbols. No other animal has such a complex symbolic language that must be learned. Animal language is largely instinctive, while *the basic human language is learned speech,* composed of sounds that symbolize things, ideas, actions, and the like. The word *table,* for example, means a raised slab because we have agreed that it will be the symbol for what we know a table to be. Otherwise, there is nothing at all "tablish" about the sound of the word. Written language uses letters or other signs to stand for the sounds of speech.

We learn to read, often with considerable effort, by noticing or being taught that groups of letters stand for the sounds that we already know how to speak. We learn to write, with even greater effort, by learning to form the letters, which are symbols of sounds, and to put them together on paper so that others can read what we "say."

Since human language is a form of human behavior, there is nothing absolute about it. It has developed slowly throughout human history and will continue to develop. No genuine language ever changes radically or rapidly; it is stable and modifies gradually to meet new tastes and conditions (see SLANG, 144).

In the English language there are perhaps 600,000 words, possibly more, but most of them are known only to specialists and are rarely used. The average mature person has a *use vocabulary* of about 10,000 words and a *recognition vocabulary* of 30,000 to 40,000. New words frequently enter a language from science, slang, or invention, from other languages, or because of new conditions and experiences; some old words drop out (become *obsolete* or *archaic*). But the vast bulk of the language remains stable.

In the world there are perhaps 2,000 spoken languages. Only thirteen of them have 50 million speakers or more. Those spoken by the largest number of people are Chinese, English, Hindustani, Spanish, and Russian. English is the language most widely scattered over the world, although Chinese has many more speakers.

84. Letters

A. *Friendly letters*

You probably need no help in writing letters to your friends. You either write letters or you don't, and how you write each depends on your relationship with the particular friend. However, there is something to be said for using the conventional form, since it gives your correspondent the information necessary for a reply. One "correct" form is on page 74.

B. *Invitations*

If you are sending invitations to a party or some other event, be sure to include all the vital information: where, when (not only the date but also the day of the week), what time the party will begin and end, and where and how to reply.

When you receive a social invitation, be sure to answer, and answer promptly. If the invitation includes the letters R.S.V.P. followed by an address, *write* a reply as directed. If R.S.V.P. is followed by a telephone number, a *telephoned* reply is proper. "R.S.V.P." is the conventional way of indicating, "Please reply." It is an abbreviation of the French *Répondez s'il vous plaît.*

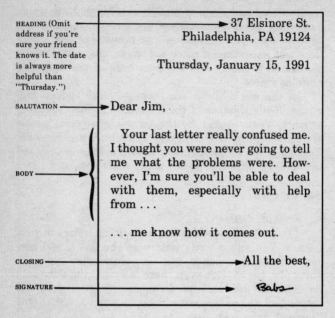

HEADING (Omit address if you're sure your friend knows it. The date is always more helpful than "Thursday.")

> 37 Elsinore St.
> Philadelphia, PA 19124
>
> Thursday, January 15, 1991

SALUTATION

Dear Jim,

BODY

Your last letter really confused me. I thought you were never going to tell me what the problems were. However, I'm sure you'll be able to deal with them, especially with help from . . .

. . . me know how it comes out.

CLOSING

All the best,

SIGNATURE

Babs

C. *Business letters*

You should be less casual in writing business letters than in correspondence with friends. If you are really serious about the business at hand—applying for a job, making a suggestion, ordering merchandise, getting satisfaction of a complaint, making an appointment to sell goods or services—you are likely to be most successful if you use a correct form (p. 75), get right to the point, stick to it, and stop when you're done. Otherwise your business reader may judge you unkindly and be less receptive to your purpose. If you can, type your letters. In any case, make sure that they are legible. It's a good idea to keep a carbon copy or photocopy for reference.

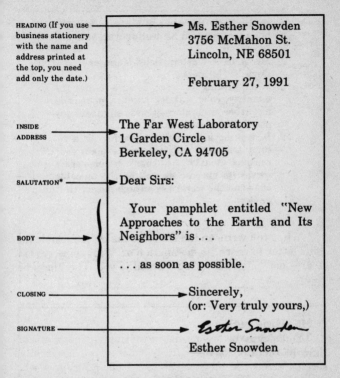

HEADING (If you use business stationery with the name and address printed at the top, you need add only the date.)

Ms. Esther Snowden
3756 McMahon St.
Lincoln, NE 68501

February 27, 1991

INSIDE ADDRESS

The Far West Laboratory
1 Garden Circle
Berkeley, CA 94705

SALUTATION*

Dear Sirs:

BODY

Your pamphlet entitled "New Approaches to the Earth and Its Neighbors" is . . .

. . . as soon as possible.

CLOSING

Sincerely,
(or: Very truly yours,)

SIGNATURE

Esther Snowden

Esther Snowden

(Typing your name below your signature ensures legibility. If you are female, the person who answers may want to know whether to address you as Miss or Mrs. If you don't care to reveal your marital status, use Ms.)

*Salutation: Business is still somewhat a man's world. Hence the "Sirs." In olden days letters were sometimes addressed "Dear Sir or Madam as the case may be." This is ponderous and isn't done any longer. If you don't want to assume that management is masculine, you may write, "Dear Friends."

L

NOTES:

1. If you know the name of the person in the business who will be dealing with your letter, use it:

   Mr. John G. Masters, Sales Manager
   Dear Mr. Masters:

2. When placing an order, be sure to give the quantity, color, catalog number, price, and any other vital information to eliminate any possibility of mistake.

3. In making a complaint or asking for a refund, keep a friendly tone and explain your reasons clearly. An angry letter rarely serves its purpose as well as a reasonable one—and the world has enough misery in it anyway.

D. *Envelopes*

What you write on the envelope makes it possible for your letter to reach its destination or, if for some reason it does not, allows it to be returned to you. Therefore, be clear.

Ms. Alicia Link
375 Jacob Ave.
Quakake, PA 18245

       Mr. Francis Smithers
       Sales Manager
       The Tryon Hose Company
       62 South Smith St.
       Manchester, MO 63011

It is permissible to put the return address on the back flap of the envelope of a friendly letter or social invitation, although it makes it a little harder for the people at the post office if they must return the letter to you.

So that it would be possible for the electronic mail-sorting machines to do their work more quickly and correctly, in 1990 the U.S. Postal Service issued new instructions about how best to address envelopes. You will notice that only capital letters are used and that periods and commas are omitted. This may seem improper to writers of "correct" English, but progress is progress, and we will do well to follow the Post Office's directions. Sample envelope:

MS ERIKA W FARMER
6110 ABSOLOM ST
SCRANTON PA 18512-1674

      MRS JAQCOB ZIMMERMANN
      806 S ARLINGTON MILL DRIVE APT 1A
      ARLINGTON VA 22204-2921

If you don't know the ZIP + 4 Code, just use the five-figure Zip Code. Your letter will get there!

85. Libraries

Libraries are collections of books, periodicals, records, microfilm, and other materials arranged so as to make it easy to find what is needed. They come in various sizes and shapes: a classroom library, a bookmobile, a library in a small town, a school library, a vast urban public library, a business library, or the library of a great university. Libraries are inexhaustible sources of information and pleasure. Librarians are always ready to help you make good use of them.

A. *Arrangement of books*

The books in a library are grouped according to subject. Some *fiction*—that is, full-length novels—is arranged alphabetically by author's last name. *Nonfiction* and other fictional forms are arranged by a combination of numbers and letters according to one of two systems.

1. *The Dewey Decimal System* is used in most school and public libraries. It divides all subjects about which books might be written into ten main categories, spanning numbers in the hundreds:

   000–099 General Works (encyclopedias, newspapers, periodicals)
   100–199 Philosophy (conduct, ethics, psychology)
   200–299 Religion (bibles, mythology)
   300–399 Social Sciences (economics, law, education, government)
   400–499 Language (dictionaries, grammars, languages)
   500–599 Pure Sciences (mathematics, physics, chemistry, astronomy)
   600–699 Technology (engineering, radio, television, computers, business, medicine)
   700–799 Arts and Recreation (music, painting, drawing, acting, photography, games, sports)
   800–899 Literature (poems, plays, essays, but *not* other fiction)
   900–999 History (history, travel, geography, biography)

   Each category is broken down into hundreds of subcategories so that an expert can tell from a book's *call number* exactly what it is about:

   Example:
   923.3H is the call number for *The Age of Moguls* by Stewart Holbrook, a work on nineteenth-century American history.

2. *The Library of Congress Classification System* is preferred in most college, university, and research libraries. In this system, the major subject

classes are indicated by letters of the alphabet followed by numbers. In this system, also, each book has a *call number* by which it can be exactly identified and located on the shelves. The major divisions are as follows:

A General Works

B Philosophy—Religion

C History—Auxiliary Sciences

D History and Topography (except America)

E-F America

G Geography—Anthropology

H Social Sciences

J Political Science

K Law

L Education

M Music

N Fine Arts

P Language and Literature

Q Science

R Medicine

S Agriculture—Plant and Animal Industry

T Technology

U Military Science

V Naval Science

Z Bibliography and Library Science

B. *How to find a book*

Nearly every library has a *card catalog,* the central file which will allow you to locate any book in the collection. There are generally three cards for each book—an *author* card, a *title* card, and a *subject* card. In most libraries all cards are arranged in the catalog drawers in a single alphabetical order. Below are three cards referring to a book by Murray L. Wax, *Indian Americans: Unity and Diversity.*

The number in the upper left-hand corner of each card is the *call number.*

Many smaller libraries give their users open access to the shelves so they can find the books they want. In

AUTHOR CARD
(This card has the name of the author at the top.)

970.5	Wax, Murray L.
W37	Indian Americans, unity and diversity

TITLE CARD
(This card has the title at the top.)

970.5	Indian Americans, unity
W37	and diversity

Wax, Murray L.
Indian Americans, unity and diversity

SUBJECT CARD
(This card has the general subject at the top.)

970.5	INDIANS, AMERICAN
W37	

Wax, Murray L.
Indian Americans, unity and diversity
Englewood Cliffs, New Jersey, Prentice Hall (c1971)
236p. (Ethnic groups in American life series)

INDIANS, AMERICAN
INDIANS, AMERICAN
(SOCIAL CONDITIONS)

larger libraries, users note on a slip of paper the call
number, author, and title of each book they want and
present it to the librarian at the call desk. The book will
then be brought to you. In large libraries most of the
books are kept in *the stacks*—closely placed shelves not
open to the general public.

In many large libraries in urban areas there is an
automated card catalog. Each of its terminals looks like
a TV screen. By pushing various buttons or areas on the
screen you can find, by author, subject, or title, what
books or other items are in the library (or any of its
branches) and even how many copies are at that moment
in or out in each branch.

There is usually a section of the library set aside for
reference books such as encyclopedias, dictionaries, guides
to periodical literature (magazines), and atlases. Most of
these may not be taken out, but many libraries provide
copying machines so that at small cost you can make
copies of any pages you would like to take with you.

Do not hesitate to ask a librarian how to find a book
or how best to use the particular library you are in.

86. Lie, lay

Many people confuse the verbs *lie* and *lay*. The verb
lie means "to assume or to be in a lying position."

Examples:
Please *lie* on the bed.
The books *lie* all over the floor.

The verb *lay* means "to put" or "to place something."

Examples:

Lay that plate on the table.

Lay the bricks in a row.

Lay takes an OBJECT, 98, as shown by the arrows just
above.

L

The biggest problem people have with these words is that they use *lay* when they mean *lie*.

Example:
wrong I'm going to *lay* down for a nap.
right I'm going to *lie* down for a nap.

Another problem is that the past TENSE, 160 of *lie* is *lay*.

Examples:
Yesterday the dog *lay* down.
He *lay* there yesterday. He will *lie* there tomorrow.

If you need to know about the PRINCIPAL PARTS, 117 of *lie* and *lay,* look in a dictionary.

87. Like, as

Like is a preposition. It introduces a prepositional phrase. *As* is usually a conjunction. It introduces a subordinate clause.

Examples:
1. He thinks like a genius.
   He speaks as a genius speaks.
2. Sara and Oscar argue like enemies.
   Polly and Molly fight as divorced people fight.

NOTE:
If you can substitute the words *the way,* use *as:*
He speaks the way a genius speaks.

M

88. Marks

Marks or grades should be considered as information, not as punishments or rewards. To benefit most from a marking system, try to understand what a mark means; if you don't know, ask. Most schools provide an official description of marks—for example: A, A— = superior; B+ = very good; B = good; B— = fairly good; C+, C = satisfactory; C— = barely satisfactory; D = poor or deficient; and F = failing. Some schools use NC, no credit, instead of failing.

Another common system is based on 100 points as perfect. Typically, 90–100 = excellent; 80–89 = good to very good; 70–79 = fair to satisfactory; 60–69 = poor but passing; and below 60 = failing or no credit. Other schools use the symbols I, II, III, IV, and so forth, or Ex, VG, G, F, P, NC. Whatever the system or label, try to understand it and use it to guide your future efforts. If you get a lower mark than you expected, ask why—not as a complaint, but because you need to know how you can do better next time.

A few schools use a simple system of "pass/fail" or "satisfactory/unsatisfactory," and some give no marks at all. Many students and teachers, especially in upper grades, have found such systems too indefinite to suit them.

Often a comment accompanies the mark. Whereas it is only natural for most people to zero in on the mark ("Whadja get?")—and the mark does give an unsentimental, brief indication of where you stand in relation to the standards of the school or class—the comment is much more informative and deserves your careful attention. It should guide your efforts to improve your performance, if you need to. If you don't know how to do better, ask.

Also, remember that in any group half the members are average and below, half are average and above—and usually the average mark (or the median or middle mark) is in the B's, not the C's. You should therefore not feel discouraged if you are not above average. High marks are pleasant to get, and they may help you to get to the next level of your education, but much more important is what and how well you learn; quite often a mark cannot reflect that value accurately.

On English papers, you may receive several marks—one for content, one for spelling, one for mechanics (punctuation and capitalization), as C—B+; S—C; M—D. Be sure you know what these marks mean, for they give you a lot of information. Also be sure to make use of the teacher's comments on your paper as well as the symbols the teacher may have put in the margins. They're as good as private tutoring, and they're free!

For more on marks of a different kind see SYMBOLS TO GUIDE REVISION OF PAPERS, 156; PROOFREADING AND PROOFREADER'S MARKS, 120.

89. May, can

Many writers and speakers misuse these words. *May* means "have permission to," whereas *can* means "be able to."

Examples:

1. *May* I watch TV for another half hour? (You're asking permission. Obviously, you *can* watch TV— you know how to.)
2. She *can* read very fast. (She has the ability to read fast.)
3. The children *can* play in the street, but it's dan-

gerous and they *may* not. (They're able but not allowed.)

90. Memorization

Some people memorize and retain materials easily; some have great difficulty. A good memory is a real advantage, but it is not by any means the most important part of intelligence. Be thankful if you have, or can develop, a good memory; but do not despair if your memory is poor. You can always look things up.

What follows is a method for memorizing poetry or prose that works well for many people, although not for all. Try these steps if you are not successful with your present method.

1. Read the passage through aloud, and make sure you understand it.
2. Read it again aloud three or four times, with full expression.
3. Close your eyes and see how far you can go in saying the passage. When you're stuck, open your eyes and refresh your memory. Proceed thus to the end.
4. Now memorize a short section at a time. Read the lines; close your eyes and say the lines.
5. Try the entire passage with a partner to prompt you when you get stuck. If you can't get a prompter, help yourself out by glancing at the book.
6. Don't keep at it too long at a stretch. Do a ten-minute spurt, go to something else, and come back later.
7. Concentrate on trouble spots and on transitions from one section to another. Make use of MNE-MONIC DEVICES, 92 if they will help.
8. Recite the passage several times just before you go to sleep. You may wake up to find yourself word-perfect without conscious effort.

9. Once you've memorized the passage, say it over once a day to fix it in your mind.
10. If you're memorizing a part in a PLAY, 112 be sure to learn the *cues*—the words or actions that come just before you speak or act.

91. Misplaced modifiers

A misplaced MODIFIER, 93 is a word or group of words that is placed carelessly in a sentence so that it does not modify—relate to—the words that the writer intended it to.

Examples:

1. *misplaced*   George longed for cold weather *in Death Valley.*

   corrected   *In Death Valley* George longed for cold weather.

2. *misplaced*   She told us about falling off the cliff *in the corridor before class.*

   corrected   *In the corridor before class* she told us about falling off the cliff.

3. *misplaced*   *At age four* my father said that I could already dismantle a TV set.

   corrected   My father said that *at age four* I could already dismantle a TV set.

NOTE: Writers misplace modifiers because they write as if they were speaking, forgetting that in speech they use gestures and changes of speed, emphasis, and tone of voice to help put across their meaning. But in writing, the reader has only the words on the page—no gestures, no voice emphasis. After you write, therefore, re-read what you have written, trying to put yourself in the position of the reader, *outside* the writing, who gets his or her idea of what you are saying from the written words only. Are there ways that your words can lead the reader's mind astray? Try to read your writing as if you were a stranger to it. See REVISION OF

PAPERS, 133 and PROOFREADING, 120. See also MODIFIERS, 93.

92. Mnemonic devices

A mnemonic device is a trick to enable you to remember something, such as the proper spelling of a certain word. The SPELLING RULES, 149 are, in a sense, mnemonic devices. There are a few other devices for helping you to remember the spelling of certain difficult words. The SPELLING DEMONS, 148 list contains yet others.

cem*e*tery (Scream "eee!" in the cemetery.)
exis*ten*ce (A cat has *ten* existences.)
h*ear* (hear with your *ear)*
lon*eli*ness *(Eli* in his loneliness)
pecu*liar* (a peculiar *liar)*
*secret*ary (A secretary keeps a *secret.)*
station*ery* (is pap*er)*
*villa*in (the villain in his *villa)*

You can probably make some devices on your own— it doesn't matter how crazy they are—that will help you remember how to spell many of the words that cause you most trouble.

93. Modifiers

Modifiers are words that change the meaning of other words by describing or limiting them. The most common modifiers are ADJECTIVES, 5 and ADVERBS, 6, which usually modify NOUNS, 96 and VERBS, 168 respectively. The noun *crime,* for example, standing alone, is quite a broad idea in our minds. But with modifiers—

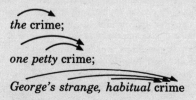

the crime;

one petty crime;

George's strange, habitual crime

87

—it becomes more precise and limited. The verb *vibrate*, to take another example, can be modified by various adverbs:

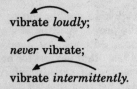

vibrate *loudly*;

never vibrate;

vibrate *intermittently*.

The modifiers affect the meaning of *vibrate*. Nouns and verbs can also be modified by PHRASES, 110; CLAUSES, 33; and other nouns:

kitchen sink.
(noun)

The subject of modification is complicated and often subtle. One can say, in fact, that every word in a sentence modifies every other word, since without any one of its parts the sentence, and all the words in it, would change. As you write, it is important, and sometimes difficult, to make your patterns of modification clear to the reader. Usually it is a matter of using your ear for language and your good sense, but sometimes you need to do some exact thinking.

N

94. Nonstandard English

Nonstandard English is English that is different from that used by most Americans. Various kinds of nonstandard English have their charms and special humor and persuasiveness. For example, in July 1989, at a rally to promote his fifth term as mayor of Detroit, Coleman Young vigorously stated to a crowd, "Ain't nobody gonna run me out." (STANDARD ENGLISH, 150 would be, "Nobody is going to put me out of office," and I'm sure Mayor Young knew that perfectly well, but he also knew that saying it the standard way wouldn't go over well with the crowd.) (See also BLACK ENGLISH, 24.)

If you wish to be considered to have achieved competence in English, you must know how to speak and write standard English. It's not that nonstandard English is *sub*standard; it's just that many people think that it is and that therefore, rightly or wrongly, they will consider you to be of substandard intelligence or ability. Thus, when you are in the world of standard English, be careful to avoid conspicuously nonstandard expressions.

Examples:
1. Where you brother at? (*Standard:* Where is your brother?)
2. I done tole you dat. (*Standard:* I've already told you that.)
3. I ain't gonna do dat. (*Standard:* I'm not going to do that—or even *goynta do,* but get that *t* in!)

4. What you-all's idea bout dems? (*Standard:* What's your idea about them?)

Be especially careful to use the VERB, 168 *be* correctly in its various TENSES, 160, singular and plural.

Present Tense		*Future Tense*	
Singular	*Plural*	*Singular*	*Plural*
I am	we are	I will (shall) be	we will (shall) be
you are	you are	you will be	you will be
he, she, it is	they are	he, she, it will be	they will be

Past Tense		*Present Perfect Tense*
Singular	*Plural*	
I was	we were	Main Point: Be sure to include the *have* or has:
you were	you were	
he, she, it was	they were	I *have* been
		he *has* been

I reemphasize one point: Using nonstandard English doesn't mean that a person is inferior or uneducated. All it means is that many people will think that he or she is inferior, and therefore the person may lose out on many opportunities in life.

95. Note-taking

Skill in taking notes is useful in several situations.

A. *Gathering information for and organizing reports*

For most REPORTS, 130 you must collect information from a number of sources, more than you could remember without notes. It is handy to write notes on three-by-five index cards so that you can arrange and rearrange them afterward to fit the ORGANIZATION, 183 of your paper. Be sure to record your sources: title, author, date, and so on; see FOOTNOTES, 62 and BIBLIOGRAPHY, 23.

B. *Reading for a course*

If you do not own the book you are reading to satisfy the needs of a particular course, you will need to take notes so that you can review the information later to reinforce your learning and to prepare for a test. Notes on reading can be taken on notebook paper or on yellow pads.

C. *Learning from a speaker*

When you want or are assigned to remember the ideas of a speaker whose lecture you are attending, notes will help. With practice you can learn to detect the organization of the speaker's remarks; you will be alert to such phrases as "first" or "another main idea is" or any other ways of pointing to a generalization, a supporting point or fact, or a conclusion. Because you may need to write key points and words rather quickly, it will be especially helpful to review and, if necessary, expand notes soon afterward in order to fill in from memory any points that may not be clear.

D. *Learning from an* INTERVIEW, 80

Be sure that you record accurately the name of, position of, and other important information about the person you are interviewing. Your situation as an interviewer is similar to your position as the listener to a speaker. But you must also think of your next question even as you listen and make your notes. Further, you may ask the person interviewed to slow down for a moment to give you time to record a major point. In interviewing, you should prepare your questions in advance—even though you should be ready to change or abandon them if a new idea comes up or if the question is answered before you ask it.

N

E. *Learning from class lectures and discussions*

Many people find it helpful to keep a notebook open and pencil poised during presentations by a teacher or during discussion. In this way they can record important facts, conclusions, recommended reading, suggestions for review, and any other important matters for later review and study.

GUIDES FOR TAKING AND USING NOTES

1. Note your sources accurately (see the first paragraph of this section).
2. Use your own words to express the ideas you read or hear.
3. If you quote the words of the source exactly, use quotation marks, and note the page of the book or the other publication from which the quotation is taken. Using the words of others without quotation marks and credit to the source is called PLAGIARISM, 111.
4. Abbreviate and condense to save time and space, but not so drastically that you cannot recall later what your notes mean. Many people develop shorthand symbols and abbreviations for commonly used words. For example, "w/o" = without, "∴" = therefore; "c" = approximately. For a report on the Industrial Revolution or on Martin Luther King, need only record "IR" or "MLK" (or even "K").
5. Note only key words and figures to jog your memory, but be sure you write enough so that the notes will not become meaningless to you later.

Example:
Passage: *"Physical addiction* is a craving for a drug, a need for it so overpowering that it becomes the addict's most important concern. He feels he cannot live without the drug and his life becomes committed to the quest for it."

Inadequate note: phys. a. craving imp. concern

Adequate note: phys. addict'n: craving, overpow
need; addict feels must have drug to live, ∴ top
concern.

6. Look over your notes at your earliest convenience
to be sure they are clear to you and to clarify them
if they are not. You may underline and excerpt
from your notes right in the margin of the page
or card, perhaps in ink of another color. This device will help fix the material in your mind.

See also REPORTS, 130; REVIEWING FOR TESTS AND EXAMS,
132.

96. Nouns

A noun is a word that *names* a person, place, thing,
idea, feeling or action. It is one of the PARTS OF SPEECH,
107.

Examples:
1. boy, cosmonaut, grammarian, Lincoln (persons)
2. Bermuda, home, school, world (places)
3. perspiration, rod, sandals (things)
4. thought, truth, religion (ideas)
5. misery, joy, sorrow (feelings)
6. walking, pushing, sweating (actions)

Nouns are used in sentences mainly as SUBJECT, 153;
OBJECT, 98; and COMPLEMENT, 39.

Examples:
1. My *dog* sank his *teeth* into your *arm.*
(simp. subj.) (obj.) (obj. of prep.)
2. Over the *fence* jumped three *kangaroos*
(obj. of prep.) (simp. subj.)
followed by a *helicopter.*
(obj. of prep.)
3. My favorite *comedian* is an *addict* and *poet.*
(simp. subj.) *(compl.)* *(compl.)*

N

NOTES:

1. Any word that becomes plural (more than one) by adding *s* or *es* is a noun: "one crutch, two crutches."

2. Any word that becomes possessive by adding *'s* or just *'* (apostrophe) is a noun: "the *ship's* propeller," "the *housemaid's* knee," "those *creeps'* blue jeans."

3. Proper nouns are special names and are capitalized: "Denver," "Denise."

A FRAME TEST, 64 for nouns is: "I am happy about (the) _____."
　　　　　　　　　　　　　　　　(noun)

97. Numbers

In formal writing, all numbers below one hundred and all round numbers (a thousand, a million) should be written out. There are a few exceptions: in dates, addresses, and tables (or sets of statistics and the like) that contain many numbers, use figures, because it can be awkward to write out even the short numbers. Numbers above a hundred, unless they are short, should be written in figures.

Example:

In my thirty-three years of collecting, I have preserved 1,035 different butterflies belonging to 106 species. My sixteen aunts and uncles and my 137 first and second cousins (or is it 138?) haven't done nearly as well.

NOTE: Use a hyphen between the words of a number below a hundred: "forty-five," "ninety-seven."

98. Objects

The object in a sentence is most commonly the word or words that receive the action of the VERB, 168. Used thus, they are called the DIRECT OBJECT, 53, or the object of the verb.

Examples:

1. Moses *hammered* his *idea* home.
   (verb)   (direct obj.)

2. His present *pleased* the *queen.*
   (verb)   (direct obj.)

Two other kinds of grammatical objects are INDIRECT OBJECTS, 75 and *objects of a preposition.* The object of a PREPOSITION, 116 is the noun or pronoun that follows a preposition and is the last word in a prepositional phrase (see PHRASES, 110).

Examples:

1. He put his foot in his *mouth.*
                    (obj. of prep.)
         (prepositional phrase)

2. Over the *fence* flew a loudly quacking duck.
            (obj. of prep.)
     (prepositional phrase)

O

99. Omissions

When you wish to omit words from a quotation, show the omission by putting three dots. These "three dots" are called an ellipsis. If the ellipsis comes at the end of a sentence, put a period and three dots.

Examples:
1. "Happy birthday to you, . . . happy birthday, dear Albert. . . . "
2. "I think that I shall never see a poem. . . . " The speaker forgot about the loveliness of trees and poems.

100. Organization

Organization is an important skill in writing and speaking. The challenge is to arrange your ideas or topics in a way that makes sense and conveys the intended meaning. There is no set of easy tricks that will enable you to organize the elements of a complicated subject, and in most cases there is probably no single best plan of organization; several can work equally well. And of course you must be able to think in an organized way before you can write and speak organized words. However, OUTLINING, 102 is a device that will help you keep your thinking straight. So will holding in mind the pattern of *beginning, middle,* and *end* (see COMPOSITIONS, C40). NOTE-TAKING, 95 on three-by-five index cards is also an aid to organizing a long paper, since the cards can easily be arranged and rearranged.

101. Origins and richness of English

The English of today comes from two main streams of language: the Anglo-Saxon (Old English) stream, spoken from about A.D. 600–1100, and the Latin or Romance stream, which is made up of languages like Italian and Spanish, but especially French. This wonderful combining of two very different streams began in 1066, when the French under William the Conqueror came over from France and defeated the Anglo-Saxons on English soil. Then French became the language of the ruling classes in England for the next three hundred years.

Thus, today, there are often two ways to express ourselves in English. We can use an elegant Romance word or a shorter Anglo-Saxon SYNONYM, 157. (Most of our "four-letter words" come from Anglo-Saxon.)

Examples:

Anglo-Saxon	Romance
spit*	expectorate
kiss	osculate
wipe out	exterminate
his act	his performance
fat	corpulent
stop	prohibit
anger	indignation
give	contribute, donate
go up	ascend
guts (It took guts to do that.)	intestinal fortitude

As a result of this wonderful language combining, English has a vast vocabulary—some 600,000–700,000 words, more, perhaps, than any other spoken or written language. And it—and therefore *you!*—can express things

---

*For an example of how to trace the history of words, here is part of the entry for the verb *spit* in the excellent *Webster's Ninth New Collegiate Dictionary*: **spit** *vb* **spit** *or* **spat** ◟spat ◝; **spit•ting** [ME **spitten,** fr. OE *spittan*] *vt* (bef. 12c) **1.** a: to eject (as saliva) from the mouth : EXPECTORATE. . . .

So you turn to *expectorate,* and the etymology section of the entry reads: [prob. fr. (assumed) NL *expectoratus,* pp. of *expectorare,* fr. L, to cast out of the mind, fr. *ex-* + *pector-, pectus* breast, soul — more at PECTORAL] *vt* (1601) **1** . . . **2**: SPIT. . . .

O

plainly or elegantly. A good DICTIONARY, 52 will give you the etymology (history) of a word. The major disadvantage of English is that its nature makes it very difficult to SPELL, 147.

102. Outlining

An outline is a systematic statement of the order, structure, and content of REPORTS, 130; COMPOSITIONS, 40; SHORT STORIES, 143; and SPEECHES, 146. The outline is usually arranged in main topics and subtopics and provides a working plan for the projected work or speech.

An outline is a tool to help organize thoughts. An informal or rough outline consists of a simple listing of the main ideas of the speech or composition you are working on, with enough space between each item to allow examples, facts, incidents, and other supporting material to be inserted under each of the main ideas.

A more formal outline, following a prescribed pattern, is carefully worked out to show how the ideas for a piece of writing or speaking relate to one another. An example of such an outline is on page 99.

Except when it is assigned as an exercise in form, an outline should be the servant of the writer or speaker, not the dominator. An outline should be subject to revision and reordering both as it is first made and also as the writing proceeds. Often the actual writing will show that the outline needs revision. In general, the PARAGRAPHS, 103 of a composition tend to follow the main elements of the outline.

A Form for Outlining

I. Introduction
   A. First point
      1. Subpoint
      2. Subpoint
   B. Second point
      1.
         a.
         b.
      2.

II. First main section of topic
   A. Subtopic
      1.
         a.
         b.
      2.
      3.
         a.
         b.
            (1)
            (2)

(Points and subpoints to establish and develop Subtopic A.)

   B. Subtopic
      1.
      2.
         a.
         b.
            (1)
            (2)
         c.

NOTES:
1. Roman numerals are used for the main topics.
2. Subtopics are marked with capital letters, then Arabic numerals, then small letters, and so on.

O

3. Each lower rank of topic is further indented.
4. The topics and subtopics are usually expressed as nouns, noun phrases, or questions; the first word of each is capitalized.

Again I remind you that the purpose of an outline is to help you organize your thoughts and topics, not provide a perfect form. When your speech or composition is done, you will probably throw the outline away (unless your teacher asks to see it in order to help you organize better).

P

103. Paragraphs

Paragraphs (except in DIALOGUE, 51) are a series of sentences that develop one topic or a section of a longer topic. The paragraph is almost always a division of a longer piece of writing; it seldom stands alone (except in school assignments!). Each paragraph generally contains a main idea or point, commonly supported by additional material—facts, opinions, examples, and the like. If there is one sentence that states the topic of the paragraph, it is called the *topic sentence,* and usually it comes at the beginning. When writing, indicate a paragraph clearly by indenting about an inch; when typing, indent five spaces. (For further suggestions on paragraphing as a part of a longer paper see COMPOSITIONS, D40 and OUTLINING, 102. In PROOFREADING, 120, the symbol for a new paragraph is ¶.

It can be good practice to develop a coherent single paragraph. The traditional way is to state the topic or main idea of the paragraph in a topic sentence. Next, *develop* the topic by sentences relating to it. Such sentences usually present facts, examples, or incidents to support the topic. The paragraph you are reading is an example of how to develop a topic.

In a good piece of writing the ideas flow smoothly from one paragraph to the next. For suggestions on how to achieve this flow, see TRANSITIONS, 164.

P

104. Parallel structure

Parallel structure applies to the practice of writing sentences in such a way that a series of grammatical elements are of the same type rather than awkwardly and unintentionally varied.

Examples:

Parallel

1. I came, I saw, I conquered.

2. He favored government of the people, by the people, for the people.

3. Let a man overcome anger by love, evil by good, the greedy by liberality, the liar by truth.
   —BUDDHA

4. My arguments are simple: it is ugly, it is smelly, and my mother is against it.

5. Because she never had been to Dallas before, because she was timid and hungry, and because she loved a man in Chicago, Jessica decided to take the next flight out.

Nonparallel (bad writing)

1. I came and then, when I saw, I was able to conquer.

2. He favored government of the people, thought it should be by the people, and done for them.

3. Let a man overcome anger by love, make evil lose to good, defeat greed by liberality, and put down a liar by telling the truth.

4. My arguments are simple: it is ugly, and the smell is terrible. Also opposed to it is my mother.

5. Because she had never been to Dallas before, and also she was timid and hungry, and, in addition, she loved a man in Chicago, Jessica decided to take the next flight out.

NOTE: In catching awkward, nonparallel passages in your own writing, your ear will probably be of even more help to you than your knowledge of grammar. Read your writing aloud to catch nonparallelisms; then correct them. However, see SENTENCES, D139.

105. Parentheses

Parentheses are used to enclose words that are outside the main thought of the sentence or paragraph or are in some way extraneous.

Examples:
1. Please order twenty-five (25) copies of the book.
2. I had never really understood what he said (perhaps he intended it that way), and therefore he remained a stranger to me.
3. My mother (at least I was later told she was my mother) left me when I was still in diapers.

NOTES:
1. Do not overuse parentheses. Commas are usually more effective. Especially do not use parentheses to insert some information (such as the name of a character in a story) that should have been established at the beginning. Instead of using the parentheses, revise the paper so that the omitted idea appears in its proper place. Parentheses can become the crutch of a lazy writer.

2. In *The Practical Stylist,* Sheridan Baker writes, "The dash says aloud what the parenthesis whispers. Both enclose interruptions too extravagant for a pair of commas to hold."*

106. Participles

Participles are verbs in the -ing or -ed form when they are used to modify NOUNS, 96 or PRONOUNS, 119 (see also MODIFIERS, 93).

---

*Sheridan Baker, *The Practical Stylist,* 3rd ed., New York (Thomas Y. Crowell Company), 1973, p. 72.

P

Examples:

verb	participle	noun modified
burn	burning ⟶	houses
edit	edited ⟶	books
run	running ⟶	water
scramble	scrambled ⟶	eggs

Very often participles are used in PHRASES, 110, forming participial phrases.

Examples:

1. *Entering the room,* I tripped over the cat.
   (part. phrase)   (pronoun)
2. The English *textbook* disappeared out the
   (noun)
   window, *hurled by an irate student.*
   (part. phrase)

NOTES:
1. Experienced writers use participial phrases (and many other grammatical elements) almost effortlessly as their ear for the words and rhythm of language tells them how to control the flow of their sentences. Inexperienced writers may need to be quite deliberate as they experiment in using such phrases, especially to break up the monotony of many short, simple sentences, uninterrupted, one after another. (See SENTENCES, D139.)
   Examples:
   1. Simple sentences:
      The puppy chased after his own tail. He wore a hole in the rug.

      Sentence with participial phrase:
      Chasing after his own tail, the puppy wore a hole in the rug.

2. Simple Sentences:
   The next thing I knew, there was Dad. He was trembling with rage.
   Sentence with participial phrase:
   The next thing I knew, there was Dad, *trembling with rage.*

The second sentence of the second example is not necessarily better than the first; it depends on the context in which the sentences appear and the emphasis you want to achieve. See also DANGLING MODIFIERS, 46.

2. Be careful not to punctuate a participial phrase as if it were a sentence.
   Example:
   Wrong: The next thing I knew, there was Dad. Trembling with rage.

See SENTENCE FRAGMENTS, 138.

107. Parts of speech

Parts of speech are the classes of words in a language. In traditional grammar the words of English are divided into eight parts of speech: NOUNS, 96; PRONOUNS, 119; VERBS, 168; ADJECTIVES, 5; ADVERBS, 6; PREPOSITIONS, 116; CONJUNCTIONS, 41; and INTERJECTIONS, 79. In reality no language can be divided neatly into eight "parts," and it is often not possible to determine the part of speech to which a word belongs until you know how it is used in a sentence.

Examples:

1. The *cook* spoiled the broth. (noun)
2. She will *cook* your goose. (verb)

If you need to know the parts of speech a particular word can be, consult a DICTIONARY, 52.

The following is a convenient summary of the parts of speech. More details about each are given under its alphabetical entry.

P

part of speech	how used	examples
noun	as name of person, place, or thing	ostrich, Mabel, destination
prounoun	to take the place of or refer to a noun	it, she, everybody
verb	to help express action or make a statement	gallop, speak, were
adjective	to modify a noun or pronoun	ugly, glamorous, putrid
adverb	to modify a verb (or adjective or another adverb)	gladly, very, yesterday
preposition	to begin a prepositional phrase	*to* the end; *over* the hill
conjunction	to join words or other elements	and, but, or, because, although
interjection	to show feeling with a single word	whoopee! ugh! wow!

NOTE: See the item on FRAME TESTS, 64 for an easy way to test what part of speech a word is.

108. Periods (.)

The period is a punctuation mark that is used as follows:

A. Use a period at the end of any sentence that is not a question or an exclamation.

Example:
My sister married a professor.

B. Use a period after abbreviations.

Examples:
N.J. (New Jersey); gals. (gallons); Mr. (mister)

Some abbreviations customarily omit periods.

Examples:
NASA (National Aeronautics and Space Administration); WAC (Women's Army Corps); UFO (Unidentified Flying Object)

When in doubt, refer to a dictionary. Words of abbreviation formed from the initials of a proper name (like NASA) are called ACRONYMS, 3.

109. Persuasion

To persuade or convince people is a principal purpose of writing and speaking. To be able to persuade others that an opinion is valid, that an idea is sound, that certain actions should be undertaken or avoided, that a given program is good or bad is a valuable skill. Three important ways that people use to persuade others are conversation, speech-making, and writing. (They also persuade by the example of their actions.)

In the long run you make the most persuasive argument when you have a good case, when you yourself are thoroughly convinced of it, and when you present your arguments with sincerity and in a well-organized manner. There are some devices—or even tricks—you can use. They can help your cause, but they won't (or shouldn't, anyway) make a bad case good. (See also DEBATING, 49)

The first step in developing a persuasive case is to *analyze the subject.* You should know all the arguments pro and con, perhaps listing them in two columns. Be sure that the arguments you use are relevant or pertinent to your case, that they do not wander off onto other subjects.

You will probably need to gather information and ideas through reading and talking with people. Don't ignore facts and ideas that go against your case, since the people you are trying to persuade may well know of them; if you are unaware of the opposing material, you weaken your argument. Take notes (see NOTE-TAKING, 95).

P

When you have gathered your material, or as you gather it, you will need to organize it. See OUTLINING, 102 and ORGANIZATION, 100.

Some methods that can be useful in persuading others are listed below.

1. *Citing facts* to support your view, naming their sources if the facts are likely to be doubted.
2. *Relating relevant incidents or experiences* in which you or others have been involved. A vividly told experience is memorable and convincing, perhaps more so than it should be.
3. *Citing authorities* who support your view—a famous doctor on a medical question, a respected teacher or principal on an educational question, and the like. Brief direct quotations from the authority are impressive.
4. *Using humor* and *funny stories* to hold the interest of your readers or listeners. Be sure, however, that you don't drag in a joke simply to get a laugh. The funny story should illustrate your argument in a memorable way.*
5. *Using association* to establish a link between things everyone likes (nice people, good feelings, love, sunny and warm places, adventure, and so on) and the point of view for which you are arguing; or associating the opposing point of view with things people don't like (murder, hate, cold, dark places, and so forth). Be careful, however, when you use association, since the device can be merely a cheap propaganda trick, somewhat dishonest, and is likely to backfire.

---

*I have written two books of humorous stories that will help you do this: *A Treasury of Humor* (Ivy Books) and *Humorous Stories About the Human Condition* (Prometheus Books).

6. *Making a direct appeal,* once you have established your case, by expressing your conviction with sincerity and feeling.

7. *Appealing to emotions,* if the subject is one you feel deeply about. Sharing your emotion with the audience in an effort to arouse your listeners' or readers' feelings can strengthen the impact of your case. Don't, however, let the emotion drown the thinking.

110. Phrases

A phrase is a group of words related in some way (often acting in a sentence as a single PART OF SPEECH, 107) and not containing a SUBJECT, 153 and VERB, 168. CLAUSES, 33 and SENTENCES, 139 do contain subjects and verbs; phrases generally do not. There are four main types of phrases in English: prepositional, participial, appositive, and verb phrases.

A. *The prepositional phrase* starts with a PREPOSITION, 116 and ends with its object.

Example:
The rock band fell *through* the *floor*.
               (prep.)   (obj. of prep.)

A prepositional phrase may be used as an adjective (modifying a noun) or as an adverb (modifying a verb).

Examples:

1. adjective phrase: The boys *on the roof*
                  (noun)   (adj. phrase)
   shouted obscenities.

2. adverb phrase: Tom ate *on the roof.*
             (verb)   (adv. phrase)

B. *The participial phrase* starts with a participle and contains words that relate to it.

P

Examples:

Seeing his baby brother, George hid the balloon.

There was Mary, *flirting with the seniors again.*

As you can see, participial phrases modify nouns and thus are adjective phrases. (See also DANGLING MODIFIERS, 46.)

C. *The appositive phrase* is a group of words that follows a noun and gives information about the noun. (See also APPOSITIVES, 20.)

Example:
Politics, *a noble profession,* is the art of the possible.
(noun)   (appos. phrase)

D. *The verb phrase* is a main verb and the auxiliaries (or helping verbs) that go with it.

Example:
They *had been weeping* silently until someone
     (aux.) (aux.) (main vb.)
gave them ten dollars.

> NOTE: Another type is the *transitional phrase* (see TRANSITIONS, 164), which helps carry the mind of the reader or listener from one section of a paper or speech to the next.
> *Examples:*
> on the other hand, in a similar way, at the same time.

See also GERUND PHRASES, 65; INFINITIVE PHRASES, 77.

111. Plagiarism

Plagiarism is the act of appropriating and passing off as one's own the words or ideas of another person. Copying another person's paper, taking the ideas from a TV program and using them without giving credit to the source, and lifting passages from an article or encyclopedia for use in a report are examples of plagiarism.

In NOTE-TAKING, 95 and in reading for REPORTS, 130, be sure to make an exact record of where your ideas come from. If you quote directly from a work, use quotation marks and identify your source in the text of the paper or in a FOOTNOTE, 62. When you express an idea that is not common knowledge, an idea that you found in your reading, you should inform your reader of the source even if you express the information in your own words (paraphrase it).

Plagiarism is quite common in schools, especially in the writing of reports. It is likely that much of it results from ignorance of the proper procedures rather than from the intent to be dishonest.

112. Plays

A play, or drama, is a literary form in which the words and actions of actors on a stage convey a true or invented story to an audience. It takes special skill to write dialogue for a play in a way that will seem real or will achieve the effect you desire. It is fun and a good chance to practice various skills to write short skits or dramatic scenes to be acted in class or at another gathering.

When writing a play or a scene, you may find it helpful to follow a standard form. Obviously, in a real play no scene would be as brief, and probably not as inconsequential, as the following one, which is given here just to exhibit the standard form.

THE CART BEFORE THE HORSE

Cast of Characters

CULLY MILLER, an ice-cream-parlor operator
JEZEBEL, his daughter
FRANKLIN, a neighborhood horse
MAYELLA, driver of the cart

Place and time: A small town in upper New York state, about 1890, midsummer.

P

On the sidewalk just outside Cully's Ice-Cream Parlor. It is late afternoon. Three small tables, each with two chairs, are placed in front of store window. At rise: CULLY MILLER, *about 55, weary and perspiring, stands down center, looking discouraged.*

CULLY *(after a moment of silent slouching and a deep sigh).* I might as well give up. Without ice, how can I make ice cream? Without ice cream—

JEZEBEL *(running in from left and shouting).* Father! Father! I have found a supply of ice.

CULLY. Go away.
(They look at each other silently for a moment, CULLY *in weary discouragement,* JEZEBEL *excited but let down by her father's response.)*

JEZEBEL *(slowly crossing and sitting in chair, right).* But, Father, listen. Mayella and Franklin are coming. They're only half a block away.

CURTAIN

In most school situations, any plays or scenes you write will probably be performed informally—without stage, curtain, or scenery. A few *properties* (props) and a suggestion or two of *costume* will be all that is needed. If the acting is good, the imagination of the audience can perform wonders. Instead of scenery you may use a *narrator,* who will tell the audience what scene they are to imagine. The narrator can also tell the audience whatever they need to know as the play proceeds from scene to scene or from one period of time to another. (A famous example of the use of a narrator is in Thornton Wilder's play *Our Town.*)

In writing *stage directions,* you will need to tell the actors and scenery designers where to move or to place objects. Directions (left, right, center) are always given from the point of view of the actors, not the audience. *Upstage* means away from the audience, *downstage* means toward the audience.

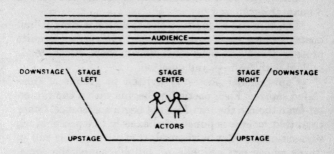

113. Plurals

Plural means more than one, as distinguished from *singular*, one only. Most nouns in English form their plural by adding *s* (boy, boys); words ending in *s, sh, ch,* and *x* add *es* (box, box*es*; church, church*es*). Most, but not all, nouns ending in *o* add *es* for the plural (hero, hero*es*; potato, potato*es*). Some words form their plurals in irregular ways (child, children; louse, lice). To find the correct plural of a word, consult a dictionary. Words ending in *y* present special problems; most commonly the *y* changes to *ies* (baby, bab*ies*).

114. Poetry

Poetry is a kind of writing, generally rhythmic, designed to convey to the reader or hearer a vivid, imaginative sense of experience. Some characteristics of poetry are:

- use of condensed language
- use of words chosen for their sound and power of suggestion
- use of FIGURATIVE LANGUAGE, 61

- use of rhyme
- use of meter (measured rhythm or beat).

One great poet, Robert Frost, explained, "Poetry is a *made* thing."

The opposite of poetry is *prose,* which is simply "not poetry." Some prose is quite poetic, some poetry is quite prosaic—there's no clear line between them. Poetry tends to deal with feelings and emotion.

Conventional poetry is written in groups of lines called *stanzas.* Each poetic line begins with a capital letter even though the line does not begin a sentence. Other than that, poetry is punctuated exactly like prose. Much conventional poetry is rhymed; that is, the lines end in words whose last syllables or syllable sound the same, except for the opening letter. It is also *metric;* that is, the lines have a more or less regular beat. The following poem illustrates all these characteristics.

Dust of Snow

The way a crow	1
Shook down on me	2
The dust of snow	3
From a hemlock tree	4
Has given my heart	5
A change of mood	6
And saved some part	7
Of a day I had rued.	8

—ROBERT FROST

(*rued:* regretted or felt sorrowful about)

The poem is written in *iambic* meter—that is, in *feet* in each of which the first syllable is *unstressed* and the second one *stressed:* ta-DUM, ta-DUM (Thĕ wáy ă crów). Each line contains two iambic feet, except for lines 4 and 8, which are deliberately irregular. The poem is perfectly rhymed: *a b a b c d c d* is the *rhyme scheme,* in which the sound *ow* is *a,* *ee* is *b,* and so on (crow *a,* me *b,* snow *a,* tree *b).*

Iambic meter is the most often used in poetry because the English language falls rather naturally into that pattern. Try reading this prose sentence aloud, emphasizing the meter (Put the accent on each syllable marked ˙.): Nŏw ás yŏu réad thĭs bóok yŏu'll sée thăt ít ĭs bést tŏ cóncĕntráte oň tópĭcs thát yŏu néed tŏ leárn aňd leáve the rést ălóne.

The second most common meter is *trochaic,* in which the feet go DUM-ta, DUM-ta:

> Then the little Hiawatha
> Learned of every bird its language

When poetry is rhymed and metered, it is called *bound verse*; when it has meter but no rhyme, it is called *blank verse*; when it is neither rhymed nor metered, it is *free verse.* It requires time and craftsmanship to write good bound or blank verse. Bad bound verse is about as bad as anything can be—the rhymes are forced, and the meter gets in the way of the ideas and feeling. Don't think that just because you've written a couple of lines that rhyme, you've made a poem. For example:

> You have in front of you this lovely book,
> And all you have to do is look and look.

This is not poetry; it's merely two metered lines that rhyme. It has none of the other characteristics of poetry. Inexperienced writers are likely to do better with free verse, which leaves them more freedom to concentrate on ideas, feelings, metaphor, and vigor.

When you read poetry aloud, you should read it slowly (it's condensed and cannot be absorbed rapidly like prose); you should not stress the rhyme and meter but read for the meaning and let the rhyme and meter take care of themselves; and you should hold your voice up at the end of the lines unless the punctuation or sense shows

P

that a sentence has ended. For example, the entire poem "Dust of Snow" is a single sentence, and it should be read accordingly, perhaps with the very slightest stress on the rhymed words but no full stop after any line because the sense does not come to an ending until the word "rued."

There is a special kind of poetry—or perhaps it should be called jingle—called a *limerick*, named after Limerick, Ireland. It is a humorous form in which the *one* verse always has five lines, rhymed *a a b b a*. The limerick's meter always (except for special surprise comic effect) is like that in the following by Edward Lear (1812–1888):

> Thĕre w̆as ăn Ŏld M̆an wĭth ă beárd,
> Whŏ sáid, "Ĭt ĭš júst ăš Ĭ feáred!—
> Tw̆o Ŏwls ănd ă Hén, foŭr Lárks ănd ă Wŕen,
> Hăv̆e áll bŭilt thĕir nésts ĭn m̆y̆ beárd!"

115. Prefixes

A prefix is a syllable or syllables added to the beginning of a word to change its meaning. Prefixes are one of the elements that make up many words, others being suffixes and roots. Most prefixes in English have their origin in Greek or Latin. It will help you to figure out the meaning of many words to know what some of the common prefixes mean. All prefixes are listed in the dictionary.

Latin prefixes

prefix	meaning	examples in word
ab-	away	abduct, abnormal
ad-	toward, to	adjourn, administer
anti-	against	antiaircraft, antifeminist
bi-	two	biped, binomial
co-	with	cooperate, coauthor
com-, con-	with	combine, concur

116

dis-	reverse of	disobey, disadvantage
ex-	out of	excavate, exclude
extra-	beyond, outside	extraordinary, extrasensory
in-	into, not	include, incapable
inter-	together, between	intertwine, international
intra-	within	intramural, intracardiac
mis-	bad, wrong	misadventure, mistake
non-	not	nonaligned, nonsense
post-	after	postgraduate, postoperative
pre-, pro-	before, forth	prepare, project
re-	back, again	regress, reread
semi-	half	semiconscious, semiskilled
sub-	under	subconscious, subcutaneous
super-	above, greater	superstructure, supertanker
trans-	across	transportation, transatlantic

Greek prefixes

prefix	*meaning*	*examples in word*
auto-	self	autohypnosis, autobiography
hydro-	water	hydroelectric, hydrophobia
micro-	small	microscope, microbiology
ortho-	right, straight	orthodox, orthodontia
sym-	together	symphony, symbiotic
tri-	three	triangle, trisect

P

NOTES:

1. In general, a prefix changes the meaning of a word or root, whereas a SUFFIX, 154 usually changes its function—its PART OF SPEECH, 107 or TENSE, 160.
2. When you add a prefix to a root, you do not change its spelling or that of the root: *mis + spell = misspell; dis + appear = disappear.* However, over the history of our language, the spelling of a good many prefixes has changed through the effect of *assimilation.* Thus, "in-migrant" has become *immigrant,* while an "out-migrant" is an *emigrant* (from *ex + migrant*).

116. Prepositions

A preposition is one of the PARTS OF SPEECH, 107. It is a word that shows the relationship of a NOUN, 96 or a PRONOUN, 119 to some other word in a SENTENCE, 139. Prepositions are commonly used in a prepositional phrase (see PHRASES, A110). There are about fifty prepositions in English. Among the most common are:

about	between	off
above	beyond	on
according to	by	over
across	down	through
after	during	to
around	for	toward
at	from	under
before	in	until
behind	instead of	up
below	into	with
beside	of	without

A FRAME TEST, 64 that works pretty well for prepositions, except *of,* is:

"It went _____ the thing(s)."
(preposition)

117. Principal parts

Principal parts are the four basic forms of a VERB, 168: the present, the past, the present PARTICIPLE, 106, and the past participle. In regular verbs, these are as follows:

present	past	present participle	past participle
look	looked	looking	(have) looked
experience	experienced	experiencing	(have) experienced

Irregular verbs form the parts differently:

present	past	present participle	past participle
eat	ate	eating	(have) eaten
go	went	going	(have) gone

The principal parts of irregular verbs are listed in DICTIONARIES, 52, usually immediately following the entry word and preceding the definitions.

118. Pronunciation

Pronunciation is saying aloud the words in your mind or written on a page. There are some forty-three different sounds in the English language. Which of them you use will depend on what part of the country you come from, how old you are, and how well educated you are. If you do not pronounce a word correctly and clearly, people may not understand you, especially if the words you use are new to the hearer.

To know how words should be pronounced, check your DICTIONARY, 52. It probably has a pronunciation key at the bottom of all the pages on the right-hand side, and a more detailed explanation in the notes at the beginning.

P

Often there is more than one acceptable pronunciation.

Examples:

hō-'tel, 'hō-tel; ī-'skrēm, 'ī-skrēm (It originally was "iced cream"); 'hät-dȯg, hät-'dȯg.

119. Pronouns

A pronoun is a word used in place of a noun (see PARTS OF SPEECH, 107). The pronoun almost always refers to the noun that immediately precedes it (goes before it) and is so understood by the reader or listener. In the following sentences the arrows point from the pronouns back to the nouns they refer to (called *antecedents*).

Examples:

1. Black is the color of my true love's hair. She dyes it.

2. A glimpse of the criminal was all I got, but it was enough to identify her.

3. Grandma clung to the pillar so hard it collapsed on her.

One problem in writing is the difficulty of making the ANTECEDENT, 16 of a pronoun absolutely clear, thus obscuring the meaning of the sentence.

Examples:

1. Lennie and Red went into *his* house. (Problem: Whose house?)
2. Mr. Trimble told Mike *he* needed a vacation. (Problem: Who needed?)

Many pronouns change form as they change CASE, 32

and *number*. The following chart lists the most common personal pronouns in English.

Subject Form		Object Form		Possessive Form	
Singular	*Plural*	*Singular*	*Plural*	*Singular*	*Plural*
I	we	me	us	my	our
you	you	you	you	your	your
he	they	him	them	his	their, theirs
she	they	her	them	her, hers	their, theirs

Other common pronouns are:

this	few	herself
that	much	yourself
these	nobody	themselves
those	none	who
each	myself	whose
both	himself	whom
some		

Another problem of using pronouns is the need to make sure that pronouns *agree with their antecedents in number* (singular or plural)—called *pronoun reference*.

Example:
wrong   One of the students lost *their* sneakers.
                                       (pronoun)
right   One of the students lost *her* sneakers.
                                       (pronoun)

> NOTE: The possessive form of pronouns does not use an APOSTROPHE, 18 (*hers, its, theirs,* and so on) with the exception of *one* (*one's* own thing).

120. Proofreading and proofreader's marks

When a book, magazine, or other publication is set in type, it is first set in galleys, galley proofs, or first pass pages. The galleys are read by proofreaders—sharp-eyed

P

experts who examine every word and punctuation mark with merciless care to match and correct every error before the publication is printed and sold.

You should be the proofreader of your own papers. Before you hand in any important piece of written work, make yourself a stranger to it and then read it as carefully as if you were a proofreader preparing it for publication. Reading it aloud to yourself will make sure that you do not miss any words. Try to get your papers done early enough to allow time for proofreading.

When you revise a paper before handing it in, or when you correct and revise it after your teacher returns it to you with SYMBOLS TO GUIDE REVISION OF PAPERS, 156 on it, you can make changes and corrections very clearly by using *proofreader's marks,* the same ones that editors use. Using these marks will save you time, in that you don't have to copy a paper over. It will save your teachers' time, too, in that their eyes can go straight to the correction or revision instead of their having to read the paper all over again. (A lot of time is wasted in schools by needless copying. Really, a *perfect* copy is needed only if the paper is being submitted for publication or will be exhibited or if some school or teacher rule requires it.)

Here are fifteen useful proofreader's marks:

1. ℗ Delete or remove the material (letter, mark, word, or whole passage).

   Examples: In the park the wasps ~~wasps~~ stung her badly.

2. ⌒ Close the gap.

   Examples: every‿thing You‿'re my friend.

3. ⌒͌ Delete the indicated material and close the gap.

   Examples: Look̸king Her̸'s was too small.

122

4. ∧ Add or insert a word or words.

   Examples: my very _{an}room   He was _{upset and quite} angry.

5. ≠ Leave a space.

   Examples: Sally was#always#looking for a friend.

6. ∩ Transpose; reverse the order.

   Examples: English is a language rich

7. ∧ Put a comma here.

   Examples: The pig ate beans peas, and beets but he refused . . .

8. ⊙ Put a period here.

   Examples: Mr Smith loves to drive His wife, however, . . .

9. ≡ Use a capital letter or letters.

   Examples: Hershey chocolates are made in hershey, pa.

   Notice: Look before you leap!

10. ℟ Use a small (lowercase) letter here.

    Examples: Sue's Rabbit ate The Carrots.

11. ¶ Start a new paragraph here.

    Example: . . . at the end. Another major point is that . . .

12. $\overset{\lor}{\lor}$ Insert a quotation mark.

   Example: She shouted,$\overset{\lor}{}$ Let me catch it!$\overset{\lor}{}$

13. $\overset{\lor}{\lor}$ Insert an apostrophe.

   Example: It$\overset{\lor}{s}$ John$\overset{\lor}{s}$ voice that impressed Molly.

14. *stet* Let the deleted material stand. Keep it.

   Example: *stet* The bear's huge hug almost killed Gracie.

15. $\supset$ No new line or paragraph here.

   Example: He was feeling entirely contented. Never had so many good things . . .

121. Propaganda

Propaganda is writing or speaking—or both, including TV—to win over the public to programs or ideas. Its purpose is to convince and persuade to action. You doubtless have heard the expression "That's nothing but propaganda"—Communist propaganda, advertising propaganda, Republican/Democratic propaganda, and so on.

Although generally the term propaganda has unfavorable connotations, some people use propaganda for good causes, or causes that they strongly believe will make the world better. These people are trying, by any means, to *propagate* their ideas and causes.

If you are going to be a competent user of English, you should learn to *recognize* propaganda, as distinguished from sound, objective, reasoned speaking and writing. Propagandists use techniques such as name-calling, mudslinging, catchy slogans ("pro-choice"; "pro-life"), or unproven assertions to urge people to get on the bandwagon. I suppose most advertising is propaganda, despite the slogan "Truth in advertising."

It's a form of competence to develop your skills of propaganda. But try to be sure that what you are propagandizing is moral and good and not just for your own selfish advantage. (See DEBATING, 49.)

122. Proper adjectives

Proper ADJECTIVES, 5 are adjectives made from PROPER NOUNS, 123. They are always capitalized.

> *Examples:*
> *American* politics
> a *Pacific* storm
> *Chinese* cooking
> an *Indian* reservation

123. Proper nouns

Proper NOUNS name a special or particular person, place, or thing. They are always capitalized.

> *Example:*
> When my old rival *Jeff* was robbing a bank in *Chicago,* he was shot down by *Jessie Bloom,* the fiercest cop in town. But unfortunately he was saved by his brother *Jack,* from *Midlands Bank,* who arrived on a *Honda* motorcycle, creating wild confusion before they fled to *Gary, Indiana.*

124. Punctuation

The main purpose of punctuation (the word comes from the Latin noun *punctus,* meaning "point") is to aid readers in better understanding the meaning of a piece of writing, the relationships of words and ideas in sentences, and the emphasis and tone intended by the writer. Early in the history of language, especially before dictionaries and grammar books existed, writers had great freedom to punctuate as they desired, but today English has become more conventionalized. Often there is only one correct way to punctuate a given passage, even

P

though there is still some room for individuality in punctuation. When in doubt, punctuate according to the rules, and if you don't know the rules, look them up. They're in this book. See APOSTROPHES ('), 18; ASTERISKS (*), 22; BRACKETS ([ ]), 28; CARETS (∧, see PROOFREADING AND PROOF-READER'S MARKS, 120); COLONS (:), 35; COMMAS (,), 36; DASHES (—), 47; ellipses (. . . , see OMISSIONS, 99); EXCLAMATION POINTS (!), 58; HYPHENS (-), 71; PARAGRAPH MARKS (¶), 103; PARENTHESES [( )], 105; QUESTION MARKS (?), 126; QUOTATION MARKS (" "), 127; SEMICOLONS (;), 137; and underlines (__, see UNDERLINING OR UNDERSCORING, 166).

125. Purpose

If you are successfully to write an essay, report, short story, or piece of propaganda, or to make a speech, you must be clear about your purpose and the nature of your readers or audience. (See WRITING FOR WHOM?, 173.) Your purpose may be one or more of the following: to give information; to persuade (see PERSUASION, 109); to make an impression, as in a job or college application or interview; to entertain; to move to action or to stop action; to calm and soothe. As you prepare your work, keep asking yourself: Will this help accomplish the purpose I have in mind?

126. Question marks (?)

A question mark at the end of a sentence indicates a question.

Examples:
1. When will you leave the house?
2. "How are you?" asked Harry.
    - NOTES:
        1. Putting a question mark at the end of any sentence, even a statement, will turn it into a question.
        Example:
        Statement: That's a house.
        Question: That's a house?
        2. Unless you are writing a comic strip, never use more than one question mark to indicate a question, and never use an exclamation mark and a question mark together.
        Example:
        Wrong: How can I possibly recite when I'm drowning?!
            If you mean that sentence to be an exclamation, use an exclamation mark only.

127. Quotation marks (" ")

For the main use of quotation marks, see DIALOGUE, 51. Whenever you are using—quoting—the exact words of someone else, indicate this fact by enclosing them in quotation marks (see NOTE-TAKING, 95). In addition:

Q

A. Use quotation marks to indicate the titles of stories, chapters, or articles within books or magazines.

Example:
In the book *How to Live Through Junior High School,* there is a chapter entitled "The Sleeping Lion Awakes."

B. Use quotation marks around a word or phrase if you wish to show it is a word you yourself would not normally use—that you wish, somehow, to separate yourself from it.

Example:
Even the old folks were "spooning" down by the lake shore.

R

128. Reading

Reading is a subject too complicated to be discussed fully in a handbook. If you read well, you are fortunate. If you have difficulty with reading—if you proceed at a much slower pace than most of your classmates; if you cannot understand or remember what you read—discuss the problem with an English teacher or a guidance counselor and ask for help in identifying your problem and in finding ways to start solving it. Take the initiative; don't merely hope that reading difficulties will go away in time.

One of the major mistakes that people make—even people who have no reading disability—is to think that there is just one way to read. Given a reading assignment, they simply sit down and read it. This can be a very inefficient use of time and mind. There are at least five types of reading:

1. *Skimming,* for a general overview of the material or to find specific items of information.
2. *Rapid, relaxed reading,* to enjoy a story or an account of something you are interested in.
3. *Close, active reading for mastery,* used with textbooks, encyclopedias, and other materials from which you must learn the main facts and ideas. (See STUDY SKILLS, 152.)
4. *Word-for-word reading* (perhaps aloud), for directions or for problems in mathematics and the sciences.

5. POETRY, 114 *reading* (best aloud), for levels of
   meaning, metaphor, feeling, and sound.

When you have an assignment, get your mind set for
the kinds of reading that you think apply.

129. Reference books

Reference books can be a great help to you in school-
work or on a job. If you are assigned a large topic for
study or a report, look it up first in a recent *encyclopedia*
in order to get a good idea of the dimensions and main
areas of the topic. This basic information will supply a
framework for deeper study. However, *don't* be limited
by the encyclopedia; it should be a starter, not a limita-
tion.

The Reader's Guide to Periodical Literature lists by
subject and author all the articles that have appeared in
over a hundred magazines. It is quite easy to use, and a
new issue comes out twice a month, making recent material accessible. Examine the *Reader's Guide*; you'll see
how useful it is.

Further, don't overlook *atlases, almanacs,* and *special dictionaries (Roget's* THESAURUS, 162 for synonyms;
biographical dictionaries for short accounts of well-known
lives; *Who's Who* and special regional and topical editions of *Who's Who,* such as *Who's Who in the East* or
Who's Who in Education, for data on important people
now living); and *books of quotations.* All reference works
are usually kept in one section of the LIBRARY, 85. Take
an hour someday to familiarize yourself with them. They
can teach you much and save you time.

130. Reports

Writing reports is a common and important task. The
ability to compile a good written or oral report is a valuable skill. A number of steps are involved.

A. *Choose a manageable topic.*
  1. It should interest you; at the very least, you should be able to develop an interest in it.
  2. It should not be so broad as to limit you to vast general statements, which require either no special knowledge or great wisdom. (*Too broad:* "Fish"; "Industry in the United States"; "Space Travel"; "Science Fiction." *Manageable:* "How Fish Are Quick-Frozen"; "The Indianapolis Telephone Industry"; "Sputnik, the First Artificial Satellite"; "H. G. Wells's *The Time Machine*: Science Fiction Almost a Century Ago.")
  3. Information on your subject should be readily available. If the topic you have selected is of interest to you and of manageable scope but you can find no sources bearing on it, change to another topic.
B. *Collect information.* See COMPOSITIONS, B40. See also REFERENCE BOOKS, 129; LIBRARIES, 85; NOTE-TAKING 95; FOOTNOTES, 62.
C. *Organize your material.* See COMPOSITIONS, C40; OUTLINING, 102.
D. *Write a first draft,* allowing space for changes—additions, deletions, reorganization, rewriting. See REVISION OF PAPERS, 133.
E. *Reread and revise your report.*
F. *Proofread your report.* See PROOFREADING, 120.
G. *Make a* BIBLIOGRAPHY, 23 *for your report* if you have used a number of sources.

Although the most important quality of a report is what it says and how well it says it, you can enhance its attractiveness, interest, and readability by finding or making illustrations that will enable the reader to understand more clearly what you have written. If you use illustrations, give each one a caption (a brief explanation, usually under the picture) and refer in the text to

R

the number of the illustration. For example, write (in PARENTHESES, 105) "see Figure 3," immediately following the sentence that applies to the illustration.

Sometimes using a different color of ink and changing the style and size of printing for the main headings make it easier and more pleasant to follow the argument of the report. Give thought to how the text is set up on the pages.

A well-designed cover sheet with the title, the date, and your name may also add clarity.

However, *do not* fancy up your report simply for the sake of making it look pretty. Your main effort should go into substance rather than appearance.

For suggestions about the oral presentation of reports, see SPEECH-MAKING, 146.

131. Restrictive and nonrestrictive clauses

A restrictive CLAUSE, 33 is one that is necessary to the basic meaning of a sentence; a nonrestrictive clause, while it adds information, can be removed without disturbing the basic meaning of a sentence. Restrictive clauses are essential; nonrestrictive clauses are nonessential. Restrictive clauses are not set off by commas from the rest of the sentence; nonrestrictive clauses are.

Examples:
1. Restrictive clause: A poem *that has been memorized by millions* is "Trees."
2. Nonrestrictive clause: "Trees," *which is a very silly poem,* is not hard to memorize.

In the first instance the clause modifies the noun *poem* and "restricts" the meaning of the noun. The clause is essential; the sentence would not make much sense without it. Therefore, no commas. In the second case, the clause modifies "Trees" but does not "restrict" or limit it—there *is* only one "Trees." The clause is nonessential;

the sentence would make perfectly good sense without it. Set it off with commas therefore.

An easier and almost foolproof way to tell whether you need to set off a clause with commas is to read the sentence aloud. If your voice naturally pauses before the *which, who,* or *whose,* set the clause off with a comma on either side; if there's no pause, leave out the commas.

Here are two more sets of examples. Try them out for meaning and to become aware of the voice pauses.

> *Examples:*
> 1. Restrictive clause: Laura is the junior *who played a leading part in four productions.*
> 2. Nonrestrictive clause: Laura, *who had the lead part in Life at Amy's,* is an excellent actress.
> 1. Restrictive clause: That seventy-year-old man *who jogs down our street* looks about fifty.
> 2. Nonrestrictive clause: Gregory Winters, *whose wife is a grouch,* is very popular with the neighbors.

132. Reviewing for tests and exams

Since people's styles of learning differ, no one system of studying for tests and exams will work equally well for everyone. However, the following suggestions may be helpful.

> A. Assemble all your materials: texts, past tests, any notes you have taken, work sheets given out during the course, and a pencil and paper to make notes as you review.
> B. Look over all the pages of the texts and other materials you are responsible for mastering. *Do not simply reread all the materials.* Remember you are reviewing, not reading new material for mastery. (See STUDY SKILLS, 152.)
> > 1. Read each heading to see if you can recall the material that follows. If you cannot, read it (or

skim, if that is enough to recall it to your mind).

2. Read each underlined or italicized word, each numbered series or list, each item you have marked in any way. Be sure that you understand the significance of all these.

3. Look at any exercises and study questions that may be included to be sure you can do or answer all of them. Be sure you understand the reason for each.

4. Memorize any lists, formulas, or rules you were assigned to know.

C. If you have a large quantity of material to review and master, make notes on a separate sheet of paper or on cards of the main points or items. Then review these notes to see if you recall the material on which they are based. If you recall little or nothing, reread the material.

D. Review carefully all tests you have had during the period under review, and be sure you can answer all the questions.

E. As you go through this procedure, if you find that you have any questions, *note them down* and ask them in class, if possible a few days before the test. If there are parts that seem more difficult for you than for others, ask the teacher for an appointment to go over problem areas with you.

F. It is a good device to try to put yourself in the position of the teacher and think out what kind of test or exam *you* would compile to test a student's knowledge of the material. It may even help to try to read the teacher's mind.

G. Just before the test, reread your notes one last time.

H. Sleep long and well the night before the test, so that your mind will be fresh.

See also TAKING TESTS AND EXAMS, 159.

133. Revision of papers

You probably do not do your best writing right off the bat. If things go well, you may set down passages of good writing, but usually there will also be clumsy sections, things that don't fit, poor TRANSITIONS, 164, awkward sentences or sentences that come in monotonous succession (see SENTENCES, D139 about sentence variety), words that aren't quite right, and—no matter how carefully you have planned ahead—sections that need to be shifted to clarify the pattern of ORGANIZATION, 100 and make the paper easier to read.

When you are working on an important paper, therefore, you should probably write a *first draft,* which will almost certainly need to be revised in major ways. If you have time, it often helps to set the first draft aside for a day or two before reading it for revision. The distance makes it easier for you to approach the paper with a clear, objective eye. After you have made the needed revisions, write (in ink) or type a fresh copy. Or maybe if you have a WORD PROCESSOR it can make revising papers much easier.

Be a sharp-eyed, sharp-eared, sharp-minded critic of your own paper before you hand it in. Be sure to PROOF-READ, 120 the final draft.

After you get your paper back from a teacher, you will probably need to revise it again, to "correct" it. In that sense an English assignment may be compared to football practice. If the team runs a play wrong, the coach will probably call the players back and say, "That's wrong. Here's how you should have run it." After he has explained, he will not say, "Okay, let's do the next play." Rather, he'll order, "Now run it right!" In this way the team learns to perform the play correctly.

When you write a paper you will probably make some errors in spelling, punctuation, capitalization, and sentence structure, no matter how carefully you have proofread. The teacher may suggest some changes, perhaps in sequencing and organizing, developing ideas, strength-

R

ening of the argument, clearing up ambiguities, and eliminating needless repetition. Benefit from the corrections and suggestions; they are directed specifically at you. Revise your paper; make all the corrections; in other words, "Run it right!" Sometimes you learn more from revising a paper than you did from first writing it.

See also SYMBOLS TO GUIDE REVISION OF PAPERS, 156; PROOFREADING, 120.

134. Rhetorical questions

A rhetorical question is a question asked for the effect it has, not to get an answer. It is somewhat like a statement put in question form.

Examples:
You don't want to fail this course, do you?
So, my friends, are we going to let evil triumph over good?
Can you think of any better way to get it done than to start right now?

In some ways the question form is less threatening to the hearer or reader than a plain statement would be. Rhetorical questions are often used in DEBATES, 49 and in papers whose purpose is PERSUASION, 109.

> NOTE: Don't overuse rhetorical questions or your readers and hearers will become weary and may not trust you. Do you want that to happen to you?

135. Roots of words

Roots are words or parts of words from which other words grow. In English many word roots come from Greek and Latin. A common Greek root is *phone* or *phono,* which came from the Greek *phōnē* ("voice"). Such words as *telephone, phonetic, phonograph, megaphone,* and *microphone* are built on this root. You will be able to think of many English words that grow from the following roots.

root	meaning	sample words
bio	life	biography, biosphere
cide	killer, killing	suicide, pesticide
geo	earth	geology, geography
graph	write	autograph, telegraph
logy	science, study	biology, astrology
mega	great	megaphone, megalopolis
ped	foot	pedal, pedestrian
phobia	fear	claustrophobia, musophobia (fear of mice)
script	write	manuscript, description
spec	look	spectator, inspect
thermo	heat	thermometer, thermostat

Dictionaries often include roots as a part of the history of a word, printing them in small caps: "BIO-"; alternatively, they may be listed separately with a definition: "bio-." If you form the habit of looking at these roots when you're referring to a dictionary, it will help you enlarge your vocabulary. (See also PREFIXES, 115 and SUFFIXES, 154.)

136. Run-on sentences

Run-on sentences are two sentences run together as if they were one. The best way to avoid this error is to *read your papers aloud* in a natural manner and listen for the place where your voice both pauses *and* drops in pitch. A pause and a drop in pitch almost certainly mark the end of a sentence (except for question sentences, which are a special case).

How to eliminate run-on sentences (r-o): Here are two examples of run-on sentences:

wrong: 1. Mabel flew down the stairs, she was in a hurry.

wrong: 2. John and Mary eat too many peanuts they will become repulsive.

There are several ways to correct run-on sentences.

R

A. *Write two sentences.*
   1. Mabel flew down the stairs. She was in a hurry.
   2. John and Mary eat too many peanuts. They will become repulsive.

B. *Separate the two main* CLAUSES, 33 *with a semi-colon.*
   1. Mabel flew down the stairs; she was in a hurry.
   2. John and Mary eat too many peanuts; they will become repulsive.

C. *Join the two main clauses by a* CONJUNCTION, 41 (don't forget the comma).
   1. Mabel flew down the stairs, for she was in a hurry.
   2. John and Mary eat too many peanuts, and they will become repulsive.

D. *Put the ideas of one sentence into a subordinate* CLAUSE, 33.
   1. Mabel flew down the stairs because she was in a hurry.
   2. If John and Mary eat too many peanuts, they will become repulsive.
   3. John and Mary, who eat too many peanuts, will become repulsive.

E. *Put the idea of one sentence into an* APPOSITIVE, 20 *phrase.*
   1. Mabel, a girl in a hurry, flew down the stairs.
   2. John and Mary, a couple who eat too many peanuts, will become repulsive.

F. *Turn one sentence into a participial* PHRASE, B110.
   1. Being in a hurry, Mary flew down the stairs.
   2. After eating too many peanuts, John and Mary will become repulsive.

S

137. Semicolons (;)

A semicolon marks a greater degree of separation
than a comma, not so great as a period. Use a semicolon
between two CLAUSES, 33 not connected by a CONJUNCTION,
41 but too closely related to call for a period.

Example:
John was on time; his girlfriend was late.

Use a semicolon to separate items in a series in which
the items themselves contain commas.

Examples:
1. Maybelle saw a large, ugly dog; a friendly, intelligent pig; four of the cutest, quietest boys; and a
   monkey, whom she liked best.
2. To a hungry man, God is food; to a naked man,
   God is clothing; to a man without shelter, God is
   a house.

138. Sentence fragments

Sentence fragments are pieces of sentences punctuated as if they were complete. Avoid them. The two most
common kinds of sentence fragments are:

A. *Subordinate* CLAUSES, 33 *punctuated as sentences*

   Examples:
   1. *wrong:* Because Perez could not see the ball.
   2. *wrong:* After she had been under water for three
      minutes.

139

S

These can be corrected in two ways.

    1. Eliminating the subordinator will turn the expression into a complete sentence, but it will in all probability change the meaning somewhat.

    Examples:
    1. Perez could not see the ball.
    2. She had been under water for three minutes.

    2. Tie the fragment to a main clause.

    Examples:
    1. *Because Perez could not see the ball,* he struck out.
    2. She was rescued *after she had been under water for three minutes.*

B. *Participial* PHRASES, B110 *punctuated as sentences*

    Examples:
    1. Disturbed by the eager crowds.
    2. Hanging from the tree beside the house.

These, also, can be corrected in two ways:

    1. Add a subject and AUXILIARY VERB, C168.

    Examples:
    1. The horse was *disturbed by the eager crowds.*
    2. A thousand bats were *hanging from the tree beside the house.*

    2. Tie the fragment to a main clause.

    Examples:
    1. The horse was tense and irritable, *disturbed by the eager crowds.*
    2. *Hanging from the tree beside the house,* the laundry swayed mysteriously.

See also SENTENCES, 139.

139. Sentences

A sentence is a group of words that sounds complete. The traditional definition of a sentence is "a group of words that expresses a complete thought," but that definition doesn't work well because many sentences are not complete thoughts.

Examples:
1. Soon it started to do so again.
2. In this case, mine couldn't.

You can easily tell which of the following word groups are sentences and which are not.

1. that boy down the street
2. laughing in their soup, all the customers of the restaurant
3. my mother is a good cook
4. we give credit to those over eighty who are accompanied by their grandparents

The third and fourth examples sound complete. Read them again and see. They should be punctuated as sentences, beginning with a capital letter and ending with a period. But the first and second examples sound incomplete. If you were reading them aloud, you would not end them with a pause and a drop in pitch (see RUN-ON SENTENCES, 136). In the first example you also want to ask, "What about the boy down the street?" In the second you wonder, "What about all the customers?"

A. *Subject and predicate*

Sentences have two main parts, a *subject* and a *predicate.* The subject is the part about which something is said; the predicate says something about the subject.

Examples:

subject	predicate
1. George	coughed.

2. My little sister	has always been an awful pest.
3. Those men under the porch	think they are repairing the pipes.
3. We	remain too quiet in class.

The main word of the subject is called the *simple subject*. It is usually a NOUN, 96 or PRONOUN, 119. All the words together in the subject are called the *complete subject*. The simple subjects in the four sentences just above are *George, sister, men,* and *we*. The main word or words in the predicate are the VERB, 168 or verb phrase (PHRASES), D110, which can be called the *simple predicate*. The simple predicates in the four sentences are *coughed, has been, are repairing,* and *remain*.

Thus, the equation is: S + P = Sent.: subject plus predicate equals sentence. In other words, a sentence is the combination of a subject with a predicate in order to express a statement. Sentences are not the only proper mode of expression, of course. We often speak, and sometimes write, in nonsentences, especially when we answer questions in conversation. Further, there are thousands of ways of putting together sentences, as you know from your own listening and reading and speaking and writing.

B. *Run-on sentences and sentence fragments*

One of the main problems inexperienced writers encounter is *run-on sentences*—that is, sentences they run together instead of punctuating as separate sentences.

Example:
My mother loved turnips, she always made us eat them too.

For suggestions on correcting this problem, see RUN-ON SENTENCES, 136.

Another major writing mistake is *sentence frag-*

ments—parts of sentences punctuated as if they were complete sentences:

> *Examples:*
> 1. John never got home for supper. *Because he had to stay late for practice.*
> 2. *Going downtown on the bus.* We saw a holdup take place right on the sidewalk.

If you read the fragments aloud, you'll hear that they don't sound complete. For suggestions on correcting this problem, see SENTENCE FRAGMENTS, 138.

C. *Four types of sentences*

Sentences are often classified into four main types, depending on the sort of response they will probably elicit from the reader or hearer.

1. *Statement sentences* (traditionally called *declarative sentences*) make a statement, give information, and so forth. Most of the sentences people use are statement sentences.

> *Examples:*
> 1. Bears don't mind cold weather.
> 2. Music is the medicine of a troubled mind.
> 3. He wondered whether the grass was greener on the other side.

2. *Request sentences* (traditionally called *imperative sentences*) make a request or give an order. The expected response is some kind of action.

> *Examples:*
> 1. Please follow that car.
> 2. Come in and eat before we both starve. (sign on a restaurant!)
> 3. Kindly shut off the TV at once.
> 4. Get out.

S

Note that request sentences have no grammatical subject. We say that the subject is understood to be *"you."* "Please leave now" means, in effect, "You please leave now." (For example,)

3. *Question sentences* (traditionally called *interrogative sentences*) ask a question. The expected response is an answer.

Examples:
1. Did you hear the baby crying?
2. Who was that lady I saw you with last night?

Question sentences often begin with a *question word* (sometimes called an *interrogator* or an *interrogative pronoun*). Common question words are *who, why, when, what,* and *where*—as in "*Who* did it?" "*Why* did he do it?"

Question sentences are formed from statement sentences in three ways.

a. By changing the order of the words so as to put the *simple subject* between the verb and its AUXILIARY, C168.

Example:
Statement: He *will go* tomorrow.
Question: *Will* he *go* tomorrow?

b. By adding a form of the verb *do* in front of the subject if there is no auxiliary in the statement.

Example:
Statement: He *likes* Mary.
Question: *Does* he *like* Mary?

c. By simply putting a *question mark* after a statement sentence.

Example:
Statement: I am handsome.
Question: I am handsome?

4. *Exclamatory sentences* express strong feeling. The expected response is any form of heightened attention—astonishment, disbelief, instant action, or some other.

Examples:
1. What a goof I made just before lunch!
2. How enormous your teeth are, Grandma!
3. Don't move or I'll shoot!

NOTES:
1. Sentences that begin with *what* or *how* and are not questions, as in the first two examples, are exclamatory sentences, even though *what* and *how* usually introduce question sentences.
2. Any sentence can be made exclamatory by ending it with an exclamation point.

D. *Sentence variety*

A piece of writing in which the sentences are repeatedly of the same sort and length is likely to make dull reading. As you write, think about variety, about how your writing sounds. (Writing has a sound even when it is read silently.) After you have written your paper, read it aloud to hear again how it sounds. Revise it if it is monotonous (see REVISION OF PAPERS, 133). Consider varying the way your sentences begin. Start some with a single-word MODIFIER, 93, some with a PHRASE, 110, some with a subordinate CLAUSE, 33. Vary the length and shape of your sentences. However, don't drag in a phrase or a subordinate clause just because you haven't used one for a while. Such an easy out will probably just make your writing sound stilted or artificial. Have confidence in your inner ear, but *keep it listening*.

E. *Simple, compound, and complex sentences*

1. *A simple sentence* has only one independent main CLAUSE, 33 and no subordinate clauses.

S

Example:
Galahad went for a walk Saturday afternoon.

2. *A compound sentence* is composed of two sentences joined by a CONJUNCTION, 41. A comma precedes the conjunction.

Example:
Galahad went crazy in the afternoon, but Mabel remained stable.

> NOTE: A simple sentence with a compound verb does not take a comma before the conjunction.
> *Example:*
> Galahad *went* crazy in the afternoon but *calmed*
>   (verb)   (verb)
> down that night. (*calmed down that night* is not a sentence)

3. *A complex sentence* is composed of a main clause and a subordinate clause. If the subordinate clause begins the sentence, set it off with a comma.

Examples:
1. James was extremely hungry because he hadn't eaten since midnight.
2. Because he hadn't eaten since midnight, James gnawed on the table leg.

See also RUN-ON SENTENCES, 136; SENTENCE FRAGMENTS, 138.

140. Series

Use commas to separate items in a series—words, PHRASES, 110, subordinate CLAUSES, 33, or short SENTENCES, 139.

Examples:
Words in a series
We sat, ate, burped, talked, and left.
Zerilda saw her mother, the dog, and three mice enter the garage.

It was a gloomy, wretched, fearsome house.

Phrases in a series

Those beasts hunted around the garbage pail, under the house, behind the fence, and among the lilacs.

Subordinate clauses in a series

Josh insists on knowing why I talk, when I talk, with whom I talk, and whether I say anything.

Short sentences in a series

My brother washed the car, Mom swept the garage, Dad cleaned the living room, and I wrote poetry.

NOTES:

1. It is not always necessary to put a comma before "and" unless omitting it would make the meaning unclear. However, using a comma before "and" in a series is never incorrect.

2. When a noun is modified by two or more words and there's no pause as you read them, don't use commas to separate them: "It was a fine old brick house." (You can test whether you need the commas by seeing if changing the order of the modifiers will still sound sensible. If it won't, don't use commas. "It was a brick old fine house" sounds wrong, so don't use commas in the original sentence. "It was a strange, ancient, decaying house" needs commas because no matter what order you put the modifiers in, the sentence still sounds sensible: "It was a decaying, ancient, strange house." (See MODIFIERS, 93.)

See also SEMICOLONS, 137.

141. Sexism and writing

Be careful when you write not to appear to assume that all human beings are male. If you do, you are writing in a sexist manner. It's your right as a free person to do this, but you should be aware of what you are doing and do it on purpose, not out of mere habit. Here are some examples of sexist and nonsexist writing.

sexist writing	*nonsexist writing*
1. man and wife	1. husband and wife
2. mankind	2. people; human beings; humankind
3. Man is ruining the environment.	3. Human beings are ruining the environment.
4. Each child learned his lesson well.	4. All the children learned their lesson well.
5. Mr. Jones and Miss Sparks worked on the project.	5. Mr. Jones and Ms. Sparks worked on the project.

(Why reveal the woman's marital status but not the man's?)

6. The girls (ladies) all enjoyed the party put on by their husbands.	6. The wives all enjoyed the party put on by their husbands.
7. The chairman presided over the meeting.	7. The chair (or chairperson) presided over the meeting.
8. postman; congressman; stewardess	8. mail carrier; member of Congress; flight attendant
9. Dear Sir: ; Gentlemen:	9. Dear Friends: ; Dear Sir or Madam:

[*not*: Dear Sir or Madam as the case may be:]

NOTE:
It's awkward, although now considered correct, to write his/her [why not her/his?]. You can avoid the problem by writing in the plural: *Not*: Every citizen should do his/her duty and vote. *Instead*: All citizens should do their duty and vote.

142. Shall, will

Years ago, it was considered correct to use *shall* after *I* and *we* (I shall go.), and *will* after *you, he, she, it,* and *they* (You will go.). Today in the United States (*not* in England), it is considered correct—standard English—to use *will* in all cases, except in sentences where we automatically use *shall*: *Shall we yell at him? Shall I tell Mabel?*

143. Short stories

There are hundreds of ways to write good short stories (stories that are only a few pages long, much shorter than novels) and no foolproof formula that will ensure success. Most short stories share certain characteristics, however, and it is helpful to a beginning writer to know them.

A. *Characters and problem*

A story centers on what happens to a person or people (the characters) who face a problem. In a good story the characters and problems will seem real in some way. Even a fantasy will have a sort of reality about it, although it could never actually happen.

B. *Plot*

The events of a story fit together into a plot, or plan, which gives the story a point and a sense of direction. The reader's interest in the plot development is called *suspense*. Most stories keep the reader in some sort of suspense.

C. *Resolution*

The characters in a short story "solve" their problem in a sequence called the resolution. At the beginning of the story the reader's curiosity is aroused; by the end it is somehow satisfied. The story will probably leave the reader with something to think about. The resolution may definitely be a happy or unhappy one, or it may involve an insoluble problem, the resolution lying in what the characters learn about themselves or others.

S

D. *Setting*

Most stories have a setting—the physical place or places in which the events take place. The setting may be described at or near the beginning or it may be developed as the plot unfolds.

E. *Beginning*

Since a short story is short, it usually has a beginning that quickly grabs the interest of the reader. The four examples that follow are by well-known authors.

"I See You Never," by Ray Bradbury

The soft knock came at the kitchen door, and when Mrs. O'Brian opened it, there on the back porch were her best tenant, Mr. Ramirez, and two police officers, one on each side of him. Mr. Ramirez just stood there, walled in and small.

"Why, Mr. Ramirez!" said Mrs. O'Brian.

"A Wicked Boy," by Anton Chekhov

Ivan Ivanych Lapkin, a young man of nice appearance, and Anna Semionovna, a young girl with a little turned-up nose, went down the steep bank and sat down on a small bench. The bench stood right by the water among some thick young osier bushes. What a wonderful little place! Once you'd sat down, you were hidden from the world—only the fish saw you, and the watertigers, running like lightning over the water.

"The Upturned Face," by Stephen Crane [1871–1900]

"What will we do now?" said the adjutant, troubled and excited.

"Bury him," said Timothy Lean.

The two officers looked down close to their toes where lay the body of their comrade. The face was chalk-blue; gleaming eyes stared at the sky. Over the two upright figures was a windy sound of bullets. . . .

"The Hour of Letdown," by E. B. White [1899–1985]

When the man came in, carrying the machine, most of us looked up from our drinks, because we had never seen anything like it before. The man set the thing down on top of the bar near the beerpulls. It took up an ungodly amount of room and you could see the bartender didn't like it any too well, having this big, ugly-looking gadget parked right there.

"Two rye-and-water," the man said.

F. *Truth*

Although a short story is fiction (that is, the events didn't really happen), it is usually true in that it shows something about human life and experience. In many ways authors of fiction can convey more truths than can authors of nonfiction because they are free to select whatever experience they wish in order to show their truth, and they do not have to worry about embarrassing themselves or other people who exist in real life.

In recent years some writers have departed from the model of the short story and experimented with stories that have little obvious form, stories which do not appear to begin or end in any structured way. They may be a slice of life, a stream of fantasy, or a seemingly miscellaneous collection of events and impressions.

144. Slang

Slang is made up of words and expressions not used in formal STANDARD ENGLISH, 150. It usually is vivid and colorful and most of it often lasts for only a short period of time and then drops out of the language. Some slang expressions, however, make it into standard English, and slang is one of the ways by which our language grows. As of this writing, the following are examples of slang:

cool your heels	shoot the breeze
gravy train	short-change artist
stinko	thingamagig
under the influence	tough cookie

S

Sometimes "dirty" words are considered to be slang. I shall not specify here. Be careful in your use of slang so as not to offend people, and avoid it in COMPOSITIONS, 40 and REPORTS, 130, unless you use it knowingly for special effect.

145. Sonnets

A sonnet is a form of POETRY, 114 that was quite common at the time of William Shakespeare (1564–1616) and earlier. A Shakespearean sonnet contains fourteen lines and is in iambic meter (ta-DUM, ta-DUM). Each of its fourteen lines has ten syllables, and the rhyme scheme is: *a b a b, c d c d, e f e f, g g.* Usually a sonnet expresses the poet's personal feelings.

Example of Shakespearean sonnet:

Let me not to the marriage of true minds	*a*
Admit impediments. Love is not love	*b*
Which alters when it alteration finds,	*a*
Or bends with the remover to remove:	*b*
O, no! it is an ever-fixèd mark,	*c*
That looks on tempests and is never shaken;	*d*
It is the star to every wand'ring bark,	*c*
Whose worth's unknown, although his height be taken.	*d*
Love's not Time's fool, though rosy lips and cheeks	*e*
Within his bending sickle's compass come;	*f*
Love alters not with his brief hours and weeks,	*e*
But bears it out even to the edge of doom:—	*f*
If this be error and upon me proved,	*g*
I never writ, nor no man ever loved.	*g*

—WILLIAM SHAKESPEARE

NOTE:
It can be an interesting, challenging, and enjoyable writing exercise to compose a sonnet. Why not try it on someone for his or her birthday? There's no law against making it funny!

152

146. Speech-making

Speech-making is a useful skill—both in school and college, where you may be assigned the task, and also later in life, if you are a person who is likely to hold positions of responsibility in which you will need to inform, persuade, or entertain people.

- A. In making a speech, as in writing a COMPOSITION, 40, the most important requirement for success is to have something interesting that you want to say.
- B. Since you must hold the attention of your listeners, it is also important that your speech be well organized so that they can follow your ideas very easily as you go from one part of your speech to the next. It is more difficult for a listener to follow an organizational pattern than it is for a reader, since the listener cannot look back. Your pattern of organization must therefore be easily understood. After an interest-provoking introduction, you may even want to say, as you would not be likely to do in writing, something on the order of "I shall be talking to you about (whatever your subject is) in four parts; I will then draw a couple of conclusions that I hope will convince you."
- C. It is rare that a person can *read* a speech well. The text comes between the speaker and the listeners. On the other hand, memorizing the speech, unless it comes easily to you, is often not satisfactory because the speech will sound memorized and the audience may feel nervous that the speaker will forget his words. For most people the best method is to speak from a clear outline that contains key words to keep the flow steady but leaves the actual words of each sentence up to the speaker to form as he or she proceeds, guided by the outline (see OUTLINING, 102). An ex-

ample of such an outline follows at the end of this
entry.

D. It is an advantage of working from an outline
that you can look at your listeners as you speak,
and they feel that you are talking directly to them
with words spoken just for them. It is very important to look at different people in the audience
as you speak.

E. Some people use a formal style of speech, others
prefer a more casual one. Your personality, your
subject, and the nature and size of your audience
will help you determine the proper style. If you're
formal, don't be stiff; if you're casual, don't slouch
or wander.

F. Obviously, to succeed, a speech must be easy to
hear—be *audible*. If there is no microphone and
public-address system, be sure to *speak to the back
row*. If you keep the back row in mind, your voice
will almost automatically reach the entire audience audibly. Some speakers mumble and then
look up and say loudly to the back, "Can you hear
me back there?" to which the answer is, at that
moment, "Yes." Satisfied, they go back to mum-
bling.

If there is a microphone, it is best for most
speakers to stand a couple of feet away from it,
to speak across it to the audience. However,
speaking close to the mike in a confidential sort
of way can be effective, provided you stay close
and don't overwhelm it with a loud voice or strong
breathing. If you're showing slides, don't turn
away from the mike as you point out the pictures.
A small neck mike that can be clipped on a few
inches below your chin is convenient if you have
to move about during your speech.

G. If possible, use a lectern to hold your notes. A
simple music stand will do; whatever you use
ought to be high enough to let you switch your

eyes easily from notes to audience and back. If you have to hold your notes in your hands (and cards are better than sheets of paper; they don't shake and rattle), frankly hold them in front of you so that you can easily keep track of where you are.

H. You really do need to be conscious of your body. Otherwise you may sway back and forth, scratch your head, swing your arms, or make meaningless repetitive gestures. The best thing is to hold your body at ease but rather still. Use your hands and arms to make gestures, perhaps for emphasis or to indicate size or feeling; but do not gesture excessively. All unnecessary body movements—especially repeated ones—distract your listeners.

I. If you come to the end of a point and need to refer briefly to your notes, simply do it. You don't have to say "uh." If you are stuck for a word, wait until it comes to you; no "uh" is necessary. A moment of silence does no harm at all; in fact, silence often focuses the audience's attention on you.

J. Unless you are an experienced speaker, you should practice your speech by yourself. If you can manage it, you might also practice it before some members of your family or with friends to get their suggestions.

K. While practicing, time your speech. Never go over your time limit. However, novice speakers quite often find that when they finally deliver their speeches, they go faster than in practice, probably because they are nervous. Many speakers speak too fast.

L. If you practice in the same room in which you will eventually make your speech, remember that a room full of people absorbs sound and that people, even when they are interested, move about and rustle a little. You need to speak more loudly than in an empty room.

M. Two problems facing some speakers are getting started and getting stopped. Therefore, it is good insurance to memorize your first sentence and last sentence. Speak them looking right at the listeners, not sounding memorized, and you'll be guaranteed a confident start and finish.

N. The following is a sample set of notes for a speech entitled "Living in a Large Family." Notice that the first and last memorized sentences are written out and that the organization of the speech is clearly evident; but most of the outline is made up of key words or phrases that suggest whole sentences or paragraphs that will be spoken extemporaneously (not memorized):

John Krim

LIVING IN A LARGE FAMILY

I. Introduction
   Living in a large family—like mine—may not be peaceful, but I like it, because if you can stay alive, you're prepared for almost any problem you may meet in the future.
   Here are several problems:

II. Getting attention
   A. Everyone needs attention.
   B. Maybe in small family you get more, but—
      1. too easy—
         parents foresee every problem
      2. practically no privacy—
         just *you* are the focus
   C. Large family—have to *earn* it! how?
      1. accomplishing something *good*
         a. my model car
         b. repair cellar steps

---

2. do something terribly *bad*
   a. stole a quarter
   b. locked sister in room
3. have really severe problem
   a. teacher who hated me
   b. neighborhood boy beat me up
      BUT . . .
4. in between you live your own life: *good!*
   self-reliance

III. Getting money
   A. Everyone needs it too! (like attention)
   B. In large family, unless rich, supply is limited
      1. no automatic allowance
      2. you have to *earn* it
         a. how I did
         b. benefits
            (1) _____
            (2) _____

            .
            .
            .
            .
            .

VIII. Conclusion
   Thus you can see that although life is harder
   in a large family, it is better because (1) you
   learn to get what you need and thus are prepared for life, and (2) you have lots of privacy,
   more than if you were the center of your parents' attention.

O. *Announcements*

A special kind of speech is the announcement. Its
main purpose is to convey information. Unless you are
trying for some special effects, the best way to make announcements is to follow a few rules.

1. Wait to start until the audience is quiet. If they don't quiet down until after you start, start again.
2. Speak slowly, clearly, and to the back row.
3. State the essential information at the beginning (what? when? where? for whom? how much?) and repeat it at the end. Give not only the date, but also the day of the week: "Wednesday, March 11," for example.

147. Spelling

Good spelling in English has little to do with IQ scores or intelligence. You can be quite dull and spell well or brilliant and spell poorly. But unfortunately many people mistakenly believe that people who spell poorly are stupid or are badly educated. This is one reason for learning to spell as correctly as you can. Another is that correct spelling makes your writing easier to understand.

Naturally good spellers have few problems. When they need to write a word, they "see" it correctly in their minds and copy it from their mental image. They can tell if it looks right once they've written it. If it's a word they don't know, they look it up in a dictionary and study it to establish a mental image. For such people, with good visual memories, spelling is a nearly effortless process.

But most people have to work at becoming acceptable spellers. And the nature of the English language, which is full of exceptions, makes the job harder. There are often several ways of spelling words wrong that sound right.

An effective method for learning to spell words that are difficult for you follows:

A. When you are not sure how to spell a word, look it up, or ask someone who knows to *write it down* for you. *Then learn it at once*—don't just copy it. If you do, you'll only have to look it up again the

next time. Once you have the correct spelling—the model—in front of you:
1. Look at it and pronounce it.
2. Underline each syllable (see SYLLABICATION, 155).
3. Say it several times, syllable by syllable; then pronounce the entire word.
4. Be aware of any trouble spots in the word.
5. When you've got the word in mind, cover the model and write the word down.
6. Check your spelling with the model. If you got it wrong, start over.
7. Now write the word on your paper. Try to write the word again a couple of times during the next day or two.

B. Learn all the words you misspell on your papers or other assignments. These are *your* problems, more important for you than any list of words in a speller.

C. Learn the six SPELLING RULES, 149. They will help you spell certain groups of words that involve major spelling problems.

D. Learn the SPELLING DEMONS, 148. These are words often used and often misspelled.

E. Keep a list of words you have learned in a notebook. Record each word in a phrase or sentence if necessary to show its meaning. (*"It's* a nice day." *"Its* roof blew off."*) From time to time go over your list of words to refresh your memory. When you write the words, try to think of MNEMONIC DEVICES, 92 to aid you.

148. Spelling demons
The expression "spelling demons" is applied to words that are often used and often misspelled. After many of them in the list that follows, I have indicated a way to help you remember the correct spelling. It will help you

S

to underline the syllables (see syllabication, 155) to clarify how to pronounce the word and how it breaks into spellable parts. When a phrase is given along with a word, learn it, since usually the problem is not how to spell the word, but *which* of several possible spellings—with different meanings—to use.

If there are other demon words for you, add them to the list. *Don't* waste time studying words you already know.

175 Spelling Demons

1. absent absence
2. accept (ac + cept)—*"accept* an invitation"
3. accommodate (two *c*'s, two *m*'s)
4. across (one *c*)
5. affect—"How does it *affect* you?"
6. again (a + gain)
7. all right (always two words)
8. already
9. among (a + mong)
10. angle—"a sharp *angle*"
11. answer (note the *w*)
12. apparent—"Many things are *apparent* to a parent."
13. appear appearance (two *p*'s; ends in *-ance*)
14. argument (*e* is dropped from *argue*)
15. athletics (only three syllables—ath + let + ics)
16. author (ends in *-or*)
17. beginner beginning (two *n*'s)
18. belief believe (*ie*)
19. business (*sin* in bu*sin*ess)
20. busy
21. calendar (ends in *-dar*)
22. capital (a *capital* letter)
23. capitol (the building with a dome)
24. captain (ends in *-tain*)
25. character (*ch* and two *a*'s)

26. choose—"Now I *choose* you." chose—"Yesterday I *chose* her."
27. clothes—"I wear *clothes.*"
28. color (ends in *-or*)
29. column (note the *n,* as in *columnar*)
30. coming (one *m*)
31. commitment *(commit + ment)*
32. committee (double *m,* double *t,* double *e*)
33. completely *(complete + ly)*
34. conscience *(con + science)* conscientious
35. conscious *(sci + ous)*
36. control controlled
37. council (student council, a group)
38. counsel (means advice or to advise)
39. counselor or counsellor (both are correct)
40. country
41. course (the English *course;* of *course*)
42. criticism criticize (critic + *ism* or *ize*)
43. deceive *(cei;* see SPELLING RULES, A149)
44. decided
45. definitely (de + *finite* + ly)
46. description (*de* + script)
47. develop development (no *e* after the *p*)
48. different (differ + *ent*)
49. disappear (dis + a*ppear*)
50. disappointed (dis + a*ppointed*)
51. discipline
52. doctor—"Call the doct*or or* else!"
53. doesn't (does + n't)
54. effect—"a beautiful *effect";* to *effect* a change"
55. embarrassed (double *r,* double *s*)
56. emphasize—"Emphasize its *size.*"
57. equipment (equip + ment) equipped
58. exaggerate (two *g*'s, one *r*)
59. excellent (*-ent*)
60. except—"I like it *except* for the dirt"; an *except*ion

61. experience (four syllables: ex + per + i + ence)
62. explanation (the *i* is dropped from *explain*)
63. extremely (extreme + ly)
64. familiar (ends in -*liar*)
65. February "Say 'BR!' in Fe*br*uary."
66. finally (final + ly; three syllables)
67. foreign foreigner (*ei*)
68. forty
69. fourth—"third and fourth"
70. friend—"a fri*end* to the *end*"
71. general generally (Pronounce all the syllables: gen + er + al + ly.)
72. government (govern + ment)
73. governor (govern + or)
74. grammar—"Bad gram*mar* will *mar*."
75. guess (note the *u*)
76. height (ends in *t*)
77. humorous (hum*or* + ous)
78. immediately (contains *ate* + *ly*)
79. independent independence (*ent*, *ence*)
80. interesting (in + ter + est + ing)
81. its—"in *its* place" (possessive pronoun)
82. it's—"*It's* here." (it is)
83. knew—"He *knew* the answer."
84. know—"I *know* him."
85. laid—"Today the hen lays an egg; yesterday she *laid* nothing."
86. lead (means both a heavy metal and to act as leader)
87. led—"He *led* like a leader."
88. library (note: *br*)
89. license
90. loose—"a *loose* tooth"
91. lose losing—"He is losing his way."
92. marriage (marri + age)
93. mathematics (math + e + mat + ics)
94. meant (mean + t)

95. medicine (note: *dic*)
96. minute (ends in *-ute*)
97. misspell (mis + spell)
98. motor (ends in *-or*)
99. naturally (natural + ly)
100. necessary necessarily (one *c;* two *s*'s)
101. notice noticeable noticing
102. occasion (two *c*'s; one *s*)
103. occurred occurring (two *c*'s; two *r*'s; see SPELL-ING RULES, C149.)
104. omitted (one *m;* two *t*'s)
105. opinion (ends in *-ion*)
106. opportunity (p*o*r)
107. paid—"Now I pay; then I *paid.*"
108. parallel
109. passed—"She *passed* the exam; he *passed* her on the street."
110. past—*"past* and present"
111. perhaps (per + haps)
112. personal—"a private, *personal* matter"
113. personnel—"the *personnel* in the office"
114. piece—"a *piece* of *pie*"
115. pleasant (ends in *-ant*)
116. precede—"one *precedes* two" (goes before it)
117. prepare preparation
118. principal "the principal—main—idea"; also, "The princi*pal* is my *pal.*")
119. principle—"It's a good princip*le* (ru*le*) to tell the truth."
120. privilege—"Pri*vile*ge is *vile.*"
121. probably (pro*bab*ly)
122. proceed—"Please *proceed* slowly." procedure (one *e*)
123. professor (one *f;* ends in *-or*)
124. quiet (two syllables)—"a *quiet* place"
125. realize (real + ize; to make real)
126. receipt (note: *pt*)

S

127. receive (*cei;* see SPELLING RULES, A149)
128. recommend (re + commend)
129. refer referring
130. religious
131. repetition (note: *pet*)
132. restaurant
133. rhythm (*r*hyth*m*: two *h*'s, two syllables)
134. safety (safe + ty)
135. schedule
136. seize (*sei*)
137. sense—"That makes *sense.*" (two *s*'s) sensible
138. separate (*a rat* in sep*ara*te)
139. similar (ends in -*lar*)
140. sincerely (sincere + ly)
141. speech (two *e*'s; *not* like sp*ea*k)
142. studying (stud + y + ing; three syllables)
143. succeed (double *c*; double *e*)
144. success (double *c*; double *s*)
145. surely (sure + ly)
146. surprise (sur + prise)
147. suspense (three *s*'s)
148. than—"larger *than* mine" (normally pronounced th'n)
149. their—"*their* house" (possessive pronoun)
150. there—"*There* are two." "*Here* and *there.*"
151. therefore (ends in -*e*)
152. they're—"*They're* gone." (*they are*)
153. thoroughly (thor + ough + ly)
154. though—"strong, though small"
155. threw—"I *threw* him out."
156. through—"Go *through* the door."
157. to—"*to* go"; "*to* the store"
158. together—"They went *together to get her.*"
159. too—"*too* much"; "me *too*" (means *also*)
160. tragedy—"There is *age* in tr*age*dy."
161. tried

S

162. truly (note: the *e* is dropped)
163. Tuesday
164. two—"One plus one equals *two*."
165. until
166. usually unusually (Get all the syllables: un + us + u + al + ly.)
167. valuable (val + u + a + ble)
168. weather—"stormy *weather*"
169. Wednesday (Wed + nes + day)
170. whether—"*whether* or not"
171. who's—"*Who's* on first?" (means *who is*)
172. whose—"*Whose* is it?" (possessive pronoun)
173. woman (*wo* + *man*, singular; *wo* + *men*, plural)
174. writing (one *t*; based on *write*) written
175. (the longest word in the English language—just for fun!) pneumonoultramicroscopicsilicovolcanoconiosis

149. Spelling rules

There are a great many spelling rules. Here are the six that I think are useful enough to learn—even they won't be useful to everyone. Some people know how to apply rules; others never seem to be able to learn. If you can learn, though, each rule will help you deal with a whole group of problem words and situations. Don't try to memorize the rules word for word. Instead, understand the spelling problem each rule deals with. *Do* memorize the exceptions.

A. Rule 1: *ie* or *ei*
   1. When sound is *ee*.
   Put *i* before *e* (believe) except after *c* (receive, ceiling)
   2. When sound is not *ee*.
   Put *e* before *i* (height, weight)

Exceptions:
The important exceptions to this rule can be remembered easily if you learn two sentences.

165

S

1. He s*ei*zed (n) *ei*ther w*ei*rd l*ei*sure. (Contains *ei* words pronounced *ee.*)
2. His fr*ie*nd s*ie*ved the misch*ie*f. (Contains *ie* words not pronounced *ee.*)

B. Rule 2: words ending in silent *e*

1. Words that end in silent *e* (taste, hope, nerve, remove) usually drop the final *e* before a suffix beginning with a vowel (-ing, -ed, -ous, -able).

   Examples:
   tasting, hoped, nervous, removable
   Exceptions:
   Exceptions are words ending in -*ce* and -*ge,* which with suffixes produce words such as "noticeable" and "courageous." The *e* keeps the *c* and the *g* soft.

2. Words that end in silent *e* usually keep the *e* before a suffix beginning with a consonant (-ment, -ly, -ful, -ness, -less).

   Examples:
   excitement, lonely, careless
   Exceptions:
   Three common exceptions are: His *ninth judgment* was *truly* wrong.

C. Rule 3: Doubling the final consonant

When one-syllable words (hit, stop, put) and words accented on the last syllable (re*mit,* con*trol,* oc*cur*) end in a single consonant after a single vowel, the final consonant is doubled when a suffix beginning with a vowel (-er, -ed, -ing, -able, -ible, -ence, -ance) is added.

Examples:
hit, hitter; stop, stopped; put, putting; control, controllable; occur, occurred; remit, remittance.
Exceptions:
Not included in this rule are:

1. Words having two vowels before the single consonant (s*eat,* s*eat*ed).
2. Words ending in two consonants (resu*lt,* resu*lt*ing).
3. Words not accented on the last syllable (*o*pen, *o*pened; *ben*efit, *ben*efiting).

D. Rule 4: Plurals and third-person singulars of words ending in *y* following a consonant

Nouns that end in *y* with a consonant before it (examples: baby, lady, sky) form their plurals by changing the *y* to *i* and adding *es* (examples: babies, ladies, skies).

Verbs that end in *y* with a consonant before them (examples: try, cry, reply) form their third-person singulars by changing the *y* to *i* and adding *es* or *ed* (examples: tries, tried; cries, cried; replies, replied).

E. Rule 5: Adding suffixes to words ending in *y*
1. Words that end in *y* after a consonant change the *y* to *i* before any suffix except *-ing*.

   Examples:
   plenty + ful = plentiful
   ready + ness = readiness
   merry + ment = merriment
   steady + est = steadiest
   happy + er = happier
   rely + able = reliable

2. When the suffix is *-ing*, the *y* is unchanged (try, trying; study, studying). Pronouncing these words carefully will help: "stud + y + ing"—three syllables.

F. Rule 6: PREFIXES, 115

Prefixes (mis-, dis-, over-, re-, un-) are added to *root* words without changing the spelling of the prefix or the root word.

S

Examples:
misspell, disagree, overdue, reinvest, unnecessary, disappear, dissolve

150. Standard English

Standard English is the English generally recognized as acceptable, both in speaking and in writing—but especially in writing. It is the sort of English you should work hard to speak competently—except when you consciously decide to use NONSTANDARD ENGLISH, 94 for a special purpose. If you want to succeed in the United States, your chances are much better if you know and use standard English.

Remember, though, that "standard" English keeps changing, as society changes. The standard English of today is quite different from that of Shakespeare's day, and if you spoke and wrote seventeenth-century English today, you would be considered strange—and probably unemployable. Language is a form of human behavior; it is not handed to us, firm and unchangeable, by some higher power. (See also BLACK ENGLISH, 24.)

151. State abbreviations

There are two ways to abbreviate (see ABBREVIATIONS, 1) the names of U.S. states and some territories: the standard abbreviation used in regular writing and the two-letter postal abbreviation used in addresses. The following list may help you.

State	Standard	Postal
Alabama	Ala.	AL
Alaska	Alaska	AK
Arizona	Ariz.	AZ
Arkansas	Ark.	AR
California	Calif.	CA
Colorado	Colo.	CO
Connecticut	Conn.	CT

Delaware	Del.	DE
District of Columbia	D.C.	DC
Florida	Fla.	FL
Georgia	Ga.	GA
Guam	Guam	GU
Hawaii	Hawaii	HI
Idaho	Idaho	ID
Illinois	Ill.	IL
Indiana	Ind.	IN
Iowa	Iowa	IA
Kansas	Kan.	KS
Kentucky	Ky.	KY
Louisiana	La.	LA
Maine	Maine	ME
Maryland	Md.	MD
Massachusetts	Mass.	MA
Michigan	Mich.	MI
Minnesota	Minn.	MN
Mississippi	Miss.	MS
Missouri	Mo.	MO
Montana	Mont.	MT
Nebraska	Neb.	NE
Nevada	Nev.	NV
New Hampshire	N.H.	NH
New Jersey	N.J.	NJ
New Mexico	N.M.	NM
New York	N.Y.	NY
North Carolina	N.C.	NC
North Dakota	N.D.	ND
Ohio	Ohio	OH
Oklahoma	Okla.	OK
Oregon	Ore.	OR
Pennsylvania	Pa.	PA
Puerto Rico	P.R.	PR
Rhode Island	R.I.	RI
South Carolina	S.C.	SC
South Dakota	S.D.	SD

Tennessee	Tenn.	TN
Texas	Texas	TX
Utah	Utah	UT
Vermont	Vt.	VT
Virginia	Va.	VA
Virgin Islands	V.I.	VI
Washington	Wash.	WA
West Virginia	W.Va.	WV
Wisconsin	Wis.	WI
Wyoming	Wyo.	WY

152. Study skills

How to "study" is not a simple lesson, easily taught. Each person has his or her style of learning. There are, however, some routines and practices that are helpful to many people and that may help you.

A. *Write down your assignments.*

Including the date due, write clearly, promptly, in a regular place, preferably a small homework notebook, not on just any available scrap of paper. Always include the date the assignment is due. If you aren't sure what the assignment means, ask the teacher.

B. *Have a regular schedule for home study.*

Most people work better after dinner than before. When you return from school, your mind needs a rest, and your body requires some food and exercise. However, styles and rhythms of brainwork and bodywork differ.

C. *Have a regular place for study.*

Equipped with pencils, pen, paper, scissors, ruler, dictionary, calendar, and a good lamp. Occasionally, though, an escape from the regular place can provide new inspiration—under a tree? on the roof?

D. *Be certain of the purpose of an assignment before you do it.*

Ask yourself, "What am I supposed to learn from this? Why was it assigned to me?" Teachers usually have a particular goal in mind when they give an assignment. What is it? If you don't know, ask—tactfully.

E. *Skim over any reading assignment rapidly before reading it closely.*

Glance at the main headings and titles or paragraph beginnings to get a general idea of what it's about and to help you relate the ideas to the main topic and to the rest of the course.

F. *Use any study aids in the book.*

Note the chapter title and the headings of the main sections. If there are *italicized* (see ITALICS, 82) words, read them with special care. Look closely at any numbered lists of points. Be sure you know why the authors included any charts, maps, and pictures. Go over any questions and exercises at the end of the chapter; they will usually stress the main ideas.

G. *Pause after each paragraph or section of the book to see if you can recall the main ideas.*

If you cannot, reread the passage. Pausing for recall and review is one of the best ways to fix the ideas in your mind.

H. *Mark your book if you own it.*

Reading should be an active process. Don't just settle back and let the words come into your eyes and be absorbed into a sort of mental fog. Instead, read with a pencil or colored marker in hand and make circles, underlinings, squiggles, and the like, to emphasize main points.

I. *Look up new words if necessary.*

Always keep a dictionary at your place of study. After you've looked up a word, try to use it a couple of times within a day or so to implant it in your mind. However, don't do so much looking up that it breaks the train of thought of the passage (see VOCABULARY BUILDING, 169).

J. *When you've finished an assignment, think back and try to recall the main ideas.*

This is a quick way to fix the ideas in your mind and to show where you need to reread. Don't just heave a sigh of relief and close the book when you reach the last word. Try to answer any end-of-chapter questions. If you cannot, review the appropriate section.

K. *Remember, there are different kinds of reading for different kinds of assignments.*

Get your mind set for the kind of reading you think applies (see READING, 128). A popular way to improve your reading and study skills is to use a method labeled **SQ3R**; *s*urvey, *q*uestion, *r*ead, *r*ecite (to yourself), and *r*eview.

L. *Note and study all corrections and suggestions made to you in class and on your papers.*

If your teacher makes a correction on your paper or a suggestion to you in class, that's important. *Note also any suggestion made to the class in general.* If the teacher thinks something is worth taking time to mention particularly, it's probably important (at least for the course), and teachers have a way of emphasizing what they are likely to ask for on a later test.

M. *Plan your time on any long-term assignment.*

If you have three weeks to do a report, divide up your time, perhaps spending a week doing rough organization and collecting materials, another week reading and taking notes, and a third week reorganizing and writing up your report and proofreading it.

N. *While doing an assignment, note down any points about which you are not clear.*

Bring them up in class at the beginning of the next period. This is not only a good way to learn; it also makes a wonderful impression on the teacher.

O. *Learn to make a rough outline* (see OUTLINING, 102).

P. *When reviewing for tests, don't reread all the materials.*

Instead, use the study aids in the book, the marks you have made, and any notes you may have taken on your reading or on what the teacher has emphasized. You may take notes on your notes or mark them up further to summarize them. Spend your time on the parts you don't know (see REVIEWING FOR TESTS AND EXAMS, 132).

Q. *Your basic obligation to your work is to try your best and to be interested in it.*

Try not to set up a block between you and your education by saying that you're bored or feeling that the work is "stupid." You have a perfect right to your feelings, but if you let them control your actions, you may fail to learn. Instead, strive to find something in the work that can catch your interest.

153. Subjects

The subject is one of the two main parts of most SENTENCES, 139. It is the part about which something is said.

Examples:
1. *My idea of happiness* is four feet on a fireplace
   (subject)
   fender —O. W. HOLMES
2. *Few horses* go as fast as the money you bet on
   (subject)
   them.
3. *He who hesitates* gets bumped from the rear.
   (subject)

   —HOMER PHILLIPS
4. *It* looks like a dying panda.
   (subject)
5. Chirping bravely under the tractor was *a small*
                                               (subject)
   cricket.

The main part of a sentence other than the subject is the predicate. See SENTENCES, A139.

The main word in the complete subject is called the *simple subject: idea, horses, he, it,* and *cricket* in the five sentences above.

154. Suffixes

Suffixes are words or parts of words added to the end of words or word roots to give them an additional, more specialized meaning or to change the TENSE, 160. Suffixes

S

also often change the PART OF SPEECH, 107 of the word. Knowing certain common suffixes, most of them borrowed or inherited from Greek or Latin, will help you make intelligent guesses about the meanings of words you may not know. A few common suffixes follow. There are many more.

suffix	meaning	examples in word
-ant -er	one who does	servant, buyer, creeper
-ist	one who believes in	deist, Darwinist, creationist
-or	one who does	bettor, operator
-ful	characterized by, full of	beautiful, remorseful
-ic -ish	like	fantastic, demonic impish, foolish
-ize	to cause to become	standardize, popularize
-less	without	hopeless, shapeless
-ly	in the manner	quietly, disgustingly
-sion -tion	process of or state of being	expulsion, rejection, depression
-ward	in the direction of	homeward, earthward
-hood -ness	condition of	childhood, priesthood foolishness, pretentiousness

Suffixes are listed in dictionaries, usually in small capitals enclosed in brackets ([ ]) after the definition of a word or as separate entries (usually preceded by a hypen, as "-hood").

See PREFIXES, 115 for a comparison of the functions of prefixes and suffixes.

155. Syllabication

Syllabication is the division of words into syllables. A syllable is a word or parts of a word that are uttered as a single vocal impulse.

Since the rules of syllabication are complicated, the only way to be certain how a word is syllabized is to refer to a dictionary. Pronouncing a word aloud carefully will often enable you to make an intelligent guess.

When a word must be divided at the end of a line, divide it between syllables (see HYPHENS, 71). A word can be divided between double consonants usually (dif ference; Mis sis sip pi). Never divide a one-syllable word.

156. Symbols to guide revision of papers

It saves time for you and the teacher if you agree on a set of symbols to be used when your paper is read and marked (see REVISION OF PAPERS, 133). What follows is a set of commonly accepted and useful symbols. Your teacher may use symbols different from these. If so, learn them! Each symbol in the margin means that there is a particular problem to be corrected in the line of writing beside it.

When your teacher has spent time correcting your paper and making suggestions about it, it's like individual instruction for you. Take full advantage of it by dealing with every mark and comment. Ask questions about those you don't understand.

awk	Awkwardly expressed. Revise. If you are unable to understand why the construction is awkward, consult your teacher.
cap	Begin the word with a capital letter.
comb	Combine into one sentence as you judge best.

s

frag	Sentence fragment—a group of words punctuated as a sentence but not a sentence. Change it by making it into a sentence or, more commonly, combining it with the sentence that precedes or follows it.
gr	Mistake in grammar. Correct it.
H	Handwriting unclear. Clarify it.
lc	Lowercase. You should not have used a capital letter.
M?	Meaning is unclear or not what you intended.
note	Note a suggestion or change made in the text.
O	Order of words is wrong or poor. Revise it.
¶	New paragraph is needed here.
no ¶	You should not start a new paragraph here.
p	Punctuation error (p(;)—use a semicolon; p(-)—use a hyphen, and so on). Correct it.
ref	What does the word refer to? Usually means unclear pronoun reference. (See PRONOUNS, 119.)
rep	Awkward repetition. Revise.
r-o	RUN-ON SENTENCES, 136—two or more sentences run together. Punctuate as separate sentences or otherwise revise.
sp	Error in spelling. Correct it.
T	Error in TENSE, 160. Revise.
W	Wrong word. Choose a better one.
w.o.	Write out; do not use ABBREVIATION, 1 or figure.

✗	Delete (omit). (Example: The ~~big~~ large boy coughed.)
/	Divide into two words (the main/street).
⌣	Join into one word (road‿block).
;/	Insert the punctuation where indicated by slash—in this case, a semicolon.
?	Is this what you mean? Are you sure of your facts? Clarify the text.
∧	Something is omitted; supply it. (Two plus ∧ equals four.)
X	Obvious error; correct it.

157. Synonyms and antonyms

A synonym is a word having the same, or almost the same, meaning as another.

Examples:
1. nasty, foul, filthy, smutty, loathsome
2. damp, moist, watery

An antonym is a word opposite in meaning to another.

Examples:
nice, bad; ugly, beautiful; large, small; stupid, intelligent; possible, impossible

When you are writing or speaking, you may increase the interest of what you say by thinking of synonyms for a word, rather than using the same word over and over.

Examples:
Sunday was very *cold*. In fact, it was so *frigid* that the streets were slippery.
She *quivered* so much that I, too, began to *shake,* and the more we *shuddered,* the more miserable we felt.

S

If you need to find synonyms, use a THESAURUS, 162.

Sometimes, of course, it is good writing to use the same word several times in a sentence.

Example:
Dolly picked up a dime, Charlie picked up a nickel, and Ozzie picked up four quarters.

T

158. Taking notes   See NOTE-TAKING, 95.

159. Taking tests and exams

If you can excel in a test or examination, even though you may not have done as well as you'd like to in your daily work, you can greatly improve your record. More important, reviewing intelligently is an excellent way to learn the material of a course, and the thinking and writing under pressure that is required during a test or exam may be good training for such challenges in the future.

A. *Preparing for the test*

There are many ways to prepare, and you should develop one that suits your style and that works for you. See REVIEWING FOR TESTS AND EXAMS, 132 for specific suggestions that may help you.

B. *Taking the test*

Again, in taking tests, people succeed in different ways. The following practices work well for many.

1. Look over the entire test quickly before you start answering any of the questions. If there are essay questions, read them right away so that your mind can mull over them even as you are working on other parts of the test. Jot down (with key words) various points to avoid losing ideas you had at first reading.

2. Bring a watch and plan your time. Don't spend more time than you should on any question. Usually the proportion of time allotted to a question should be re-

T

lated to the proportion of credit given for it. Leave some blank space at the end of each answer in case you have time to come back to it at the end to add more information.

3. Read the directions and questions carefully. Many people have failed or done poorly on a test or exam by misinterpreting the directions or, in effect, answering the wrong question because he misread it.

4. Write legibly but not too slowly. *Never* waste time copying over an answer on a timed test.

5. Be sure that you number your answers plainly according to the numbers of the questions. Make it easy for the teacher to follow your paper.

6. Answer first the questions you know best (but don't spend more than the allotted portion of time on them) and do the hardest ones last—unless, of course, you are required to answer the questions in order. Never spend a lot of time puzzling uselessly over a question you cannot answer. Come back to it at the end if there's time.

7. Unless you're a sure writer, save a few minutes (maybe 5 percent of the time) to PROOFREAD, 120 and revise your answers.

8. If you're not certain of an answer, make intelligent guesses. This practice is especially important on multiple-choice tests. If you can eliminate one or more of the choices as certainly wrong, it will pay you to guess among the others.

160. Tenses
Tense, in grammar, refers to time, and the tense of a sentence is usually expressed by the VERB, 168. Tenses can be divided roughly into three large categories: present, past, and future. There are many complex variations, however, and most of us use tenses correctly by imitation, even though it's difficult to explain just how we do it.

Examples:
1. *Present tense:* The city is beautiful.
2. *Past tense:* The city was beautiful.
3. *Future tense:* The city will be beautiful.

An important form of the past tense often not used when it should be is the *past perfect,* which indicates an action or condition completed *before another past* action or condition—a sort of further past.

Examples:
1. The city *had been* beautiful before they
   (past perfect tense)
   bombed it.
   (past tense)
2. Molly *had loved* him before he *popped*
   (past perfect tense)   (past tense)
   his gum.

There is also the *future perfect tense.* It expresses an action or state that will begin in the future and will be completed by a specific time in the future.

Examples:
1. The new building *will have beautified* the city before the architect arrives home from abroad.
2. Molly and Herb *will have been married* fifty years before the year ends, despite the bubble-gum popping.

There is yet another tense, the *present perfect tense,* that refers to something that started in the past and is still going on now.

Examples:
1. I *have been working* for several hours now.
2. My grandmother *has been going* to the hospital very often these days.

In writing, it is important not to change tenses needlessly as you proceed through a story or account of events. Change tense only when you have a reason to do so.

T

Examples:
1. *wrong* The teacher *entered* the room and *starts* teaching while the class still *talked*.
2. *right* The teacher *entered* the room and *started* teaching while the class *was* still *talking*.
3. *right* The teacher *enters* the room and *starts* teaching while the class *is* still *talking*.

161. That, which, and who-whose-whom

The *relative pronouns* "that," "which," "who," "whose," and "whom" relate the CLAUSE, 33 of which they are the first word to another word or other words in a sentence. (See PRONOUNS, 119.)

Examples:

1. Don't bite the hand *that* feeds you.

2. I dislodged a rock, *which* rattled down the slope.

3. The woman *who* shot him was insane.

4. Those astronauts *whom* I met didn't know how to swim.

5. The dog *whose* tooth was missing had left it in my right leg.

In general, use *who* and *whom* when referring to people, *which* when referring to things, and *that* when referring to either people or things. Use *whom* when it functions as the object of a verb, or preposition. See OBJECT, 98.

Example:
... *whom* I met ... ; to *whom* I was talking
<small>(obj. of vb.) (subj.) (verb)   (prep.) (obj. of prep.)</small>

See also WHO, WHOM, 171.

162. Thesaurus

A thesaurus is a reference book of related words grouped by ideas. It contains lists of synonyms (words that have similar meanings) and, often, antonyms (words that have opposite meanings). A thesaurus is especially useful when you are looking for a word to express the precise meaning you have in mind but can't quite pinpoint.

163. Titles

Other things being equal, a composition is improved by a good title. It arouses the interest of readers; it gives the paper a label which makes it easier to identify and remember. It's worth more than a moment of your time to think up a good title or label for each paper you write.

See CAPITALIZATION, A31 for its application to titles. When writing the titles of books or magazines, underline (italicize) them; when writing the titles of chapters or articles within books or magazines, enclose them in quotation marks.

Example:
Chapter 5 of H. G. Wells's *The War of the Worlds* is called "The Heat Ray."

164. Transitions

A writer or speaker must lead the reader or listener from one idea or section to the next in a way that is easy and pleasant to follow. Paragraphs should succeed each other in some kind of comfortable progression. Often the succession of ideas and paragraphs is made easier to understand by the use of *transitional words or phrases*. For example, if you have written about one aspect of a subject and are ready to switch to a contrasting aspect, you can signal the switch with such phrases or words as "on the other hand" and "however." However, if you want the reader to understand that you are continuing along the same lines, a word such as "furthermore" or a phrase such as "in addition" helps to clue them in.

The following useful transitional words and phrases are roughly grouped by the function they serve. Notice that some of them serve more than one function.

adding: also, another, at the same time, first (second, third), in addition, in the same way, moreover, next

concluding: at last, finally, in conclusion, therefore

continuing: also, another, at the same time, furthermore, indeed, in the first (second, third) place, in the same way, meantime, then (be careful not to overuse this one), too

contrasting: but, however, on the other hand, one . . . another

exemplifying: for example, that is

explaining or amplifying: also, consequently, for example, furthermore, in addition, indeed, in fact, moreover, of course, that is, therefore, too

165. Typing

Typing is a very useful skill if you are to do well in any subject that requires a lot of writing. Many people find it quite easy to learn to type while they are of school age and able to establish habits easily. I would recommend that you learn to touch-type as early as possible if you have a serious interest in academic work. Take a course if one is offered by your school, find one in the community (perhaps during the summer), or get a book of typing lessons and learn on your own.

When you type papers for school or for publication, leave double spaces between lines (it's much easier for teachers to read and correct and for you to revise), leave a left-hand margin of an inch and a half, and avoid crowding.

However, don't become so dependent on typing that you lose the skill of writing by hand quickly and legibly, since this, of course, is what you will have to do in exams, tests, and other writing in school.

See also WORD PROCESSORS, 172.

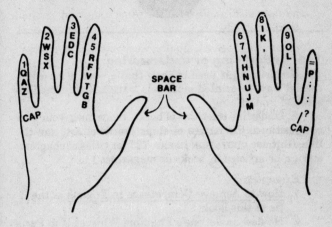

PLAN FOR TOUCH-TYPING
(This is basic. Some typewriters differ slightly
from the above.)

U

166. Underlining or underscoring

Underlining is used to show that a word is used in a special way. In printed materials ITALICS, 82 are used instead of underlining.

A. Underline the titles of books, magazines, your own compositions, the names of ships, works of art, and the like. (But use QUOTATION MARKS, 127 for titles of chapters, stories, or articles in books or magazines.)

Examples:

1. How to Achieve Competence in English is the title of this book.
2. He flew on Jetline's Phantom Whisper II to Paris to see the Mona Lisa.

B. Underline—but rarely—for emphasis.

C. Underline a word referred to as a word or a letter as a letter.

Examples:

1. He used love three times in the sentence and lover twice.
2. Don't leave the e out of courageous.

D. Underline foreign words and phrases.

Example:

If you study Latin, you'll understand the phrase e pluribus unum on your coins.

167. Uninterested, disinterested

People often make the mistake of using *disinterested* when they mean *uninterested*. *Disinterested* means unbiased or objective, having no special selfish interest in the matter. *Uninterested* means not interested.

Examples:

1. They were *uninterested* in mountain climbing or any sort of hard exercise.
2. She was *uninterested* in his offers to marry her.
3. To make a sound judgment on this complicated matter, we need a *disinterested* expert advisor.
4. When your emotions are involved, it is impossible to give a *disinterested* opinion.

V

168. Verbs

A verb is one of the PARTS OF SPEECH, 107. As most commonly defined, a verb is a word that expresses action or state of being. Most verbs express action—such as *shout, jump, crush, pound, wriggle, snort,* and *push*—as well as "mental" actions—for example, *think, believe, understand, sympathize,* and *hate.*

Verbs, and no other class of words, change TENSE, 160 by adding endings, by grouping with auxiliaries, or by changing form.

Examples:
1. I *speak.* I *spoke.* I have *spoken.*
(aux.)
2. He *listens.* They *listened.* We shall *listen.*
(aux.)

Verbs are usually the most important part of the predicate in a sentence. See SENTENCES, A139. A FRAME TEST, 64 for verbs is: "Let's _____ it."
(verb)
Any word that sounds right or makes sense in the blank can be a verb; in terms of the frame sentence it must be singular in number and in the present tense.

A. *Transitive and intransitive verbs*
1. Transitive verbs are verbs that take an object (see DIRECT OBJECTS, 53). That is, the action of the verb is received by a grammatical object.

Examples:

1. The rhino *charged* the *man.*
      (trans. vb.)   (object)

2. He *spoke* his *thoughts.*
   (trans. vb.)   (object)

3. The man *whom* she *loved* was very humorous.
      (object)   (trans. vb.)

2. Intransitive verbs are verbs whose action does not carry across to something else (a direct object) but is complete in itself.

Examples:
1. Alfred is *snoring.*
            (intr. vb.)
2. The talking dog *spoke* too long.
                  (intr. vb.)
3. Night *fell* and I *trembled.*
      (intr. vb.)   (intr. vb.)

NOTE:
Many verbs can be used both transitively and intransitively.
Examples:
1. Joe *feels* stubborn. (intransitive)

2. Joe *feels* the squishy mud. (transitive)
3. Cleopatra *loved* well. (intransitive)

4. Cleopatra *loved* Antony. (transitive)

B. *Linking verbs*
   Linking verbs, in old-fashioned grammars called *copulative verbs* (because they couple), are a special subclass of verbs. They do not express action but link elements in sentences that in some way refer to the same thing. They are followed by COMPLEMENTS, 39, completers of the sentence.

189

V

Examples: subject linking verb complement

1. Jim is a bum. (Jim = bum)
        (noun)
2. Joan became a musician
             (noun)

   (Joan = musician)
3. Jim was handsome.
         (adj.)

   (Jim = handsome; handsome Jim)
4. Garbage smells lovely to pigs.
              (adj.)

   (garbage = lovely; lovely garbage—to pigs!)

NOTES:

1. The word that appears in the predicate (see
SENTENCES, 139) and is linked to the subject
by the linking verb is called the complement—the element that completes the sentence. In the first sentence above the
complement is *bum.* Complements can be either nouns or adjectives.
2. There are only a very few common linking
verbs in English. By far the most common is
the verb *be.* You don't very often use it in
that form except in such sentences as "Be
brave"; "be a friend to me." But the verb *be*
has several common forms: *am, is, are, was,
were.* The other common linking verbs are:
*appear, become, feel, grow, look, remain,
seem, smell, sound, taste.*
Examples:

as linking verb   *as nonlinking verb*
1. The lamb *feels* sick. The baby *feels* the *lamb.*
   (complement)   (obj. of verb)
2. Soup *tastes* delicious. Bob *tastes* the soup.
   (complement)   (obj. of verb)

A FRAME TEST, 64 for linking verbs is: They _____
nice.   (linking verb)

C. *Auxiliary verbs*

Auxiliary verbs, sometimes called *helping verbs,* combine with main verbs to show change of TENSE, 160 or time.

Examples:
1. George *is   swimming* in the bathtub.

(auxil.) (main vb.)

(present tense)
2. The alligator *was tossed* by the waves.

(auxil.) (main vb.)

(past tense)
3. Mabel *will   claim* the victory. (future tense)

(auxil.) (main verb)
4. Mr. Jones *had been doing* the laundry.

(auxil.) (auxil.) (main vb.)

(past perfect tense)

About twenty auxiliaries are used in English in various combinations:

am, is, are, was, were, be, been
can, could
do, does, did
has, have, had
may, might
shall, will, should, would

Some of the auxiliaries can also be used as main verbs.

Examples:
1. Frank *did* write yesterday.

(auxil.)
2. Frank *did* his homework.

(main verb)
3. Poor swimmers *have* drowned out there.

(auxil.)
4. Poor swimmers *have* trouble with the undertow.

(main verb)

V

169. Vocabulary building

A person with a large vocabulary tends to succeed better at communication than does a person with a small one, but that's not to say that making an intensive effort to build your vocabulary will make you more likely to succeed in life. It's curiosity, interest, intelligence, observation, richness of experience, reading, listening, and good memory that tend to produce both ample vocabularies and successful people.

The average person learns most of the 30,000 to 40,000 words whose meaning he or she recognizes by hearing or reading them in context or simply absorbing them without conscious effort (see LANGUAGE, 83). The best way to a good vocabulary, therefore, is to read a great deal and to participate in a lot of good talk. We learn relatively few words by purposefully referring to dictionaries. However, even those extra few are of value, and no one will make a mistake by working on developing a larger vocabulary. Here are some suggestions of how to do it.

A. Read plenty of good books. When you come across a new word, or a new meaning of an old word, stop and see if you can understand it from its CONTEXT, 42, the words around it. If you can't, and if you can manage it without interrupting the thought of the book too much, look it up in a dictionary or ask somebody and then repeat its meaning to yourself a couple of times. Further, try to use a new word in writing or conversation a few times over the next several days.

B. Listen to good talk and be alert to new words you hear or to new meanings of words you already know. Then treat them just as you do new words you read.

C. Learn and be alert to parts of words: PREFIXES, 115; SUFFIXES, 154; and ROOTS, 135. Knowing them enables you to make intelligent guesses about the meanings of words.

D. If you are studying a foreign language, be alert for words in that language that relate to words in

English. English has inherited or borrowed much of its vocabulary of 600,000–700,000 words from Latin, Greek, French, Spanish, and German. Generally the shorter, easier ones come from Germanic (Anglo-Saxon) tongues, while the longer, more elaborate ones are derived from the others.

170. Voice

In grammar, voice denotes the form of the verb that shows the relation between the subject and verb. The *active voice* means that the subject does the action; the *passive voice* means that the subject is acted upon by the verb.

> *Examples:*
> active voice
> 1. John *destroyed* the picture.
> 2. Gloria *wanted* a medium-rare steak.
> 3. Many people *think* the idea is no good.
>
> passive voice
> 1. The picture *was destroyed* by John.
> 2. A medium-rare steak *was wanted* by Gloria.
> 3. It *is thought* by many people that the idea is no good.

The active voice is usually more forceful and direct than the passive, while the passive expresses greater caution and is sometimes awkward and ponderous (as in the second example). When in doubt, choose the active voice. Don't hide behind the passive. If you think something, write, "I think," not "It is thought that." The passive voice conceals the "doer" of the deed.

171. Who, whom

Who and whom are PRONOUNS, 119; they can serve as *interrogative pronouns*—pronouns that ask a question—or relative pronouns (see THAT, WHICH, AND WHO-WHOSE-WHOM, 161). The word *who* is the subjective case or form; *whom* is the objective case. When you use the pronoun as a grammatical subject, use *who*.

Examples:

1. *Who went* out the door just then?
   (subj.) (verb)

2. The person *who* I think *did* it escaped over
   (subj.) (verb)

   the wall.

When you use the pronoun as a grammatical object either of a PREPOSITION, 116 or of a VERB, 168, use *whom*.

Examples:

1. *With whom* did Molly share her rocking chair?
   (prep.) (obj. of prep.)

2. The person *whom* she *strangled* was never seen
   (object of vb.) (verb)

   again.

In informal speech—most of the speaking we all do—the word *whom* is gradually disappearing, although there are still many people who like to hear it used correctly, particularly after a preposition. In writing, however, *whom* is alive and well, and you should know when and how to use it.

172. Word processors

A word processor is a computer program that enables you to use the computer as a very powerful typewriter (see TYPING, 165) on which text can be quickly revised and rearranged without retyping. You can easily correct spelling or rearrange the words in a sentence. It is a simple matter to exchange one paragraph with another. Many word processing programs will check your spelling.

Good writers often write several drafts. When writing with a word processor, you can let your ideas flow on the first draft and then, without a great deal of retyping, achieve correct form through revision. People who have handwriting that is hard to read also benefit from seeing their words immediately appear in neatly formed letters and easy-to-correct sentences. Personal computers with word processing programs and printers cost several times more than a good typewriter, but they are such great facilitators of good writing—in school, college, and life—that almost everybody who gets one and learns to use it will never again want to be without it.

173. Writing for whom?

Let's face it, most writing in most schools is done for teachers. That's too bad, because most of the writing in life outside of school is done for different audiences. However, a good teacher can teach you how to write better; if you are in school, therefore, keep writing and try to benefit from the instruction you are given. If you find the instruction limiting rather than helpful, learn what you can from it and do other writing for yourself, or submit it to other people if you'd like other reactions.

You will do best in school if you are clear for whom you are writing. Discuss this question in class before starting on an assignment. Some of the "audiences" or readerships for whom you might write are:

W

1. *yourself*—as in a confidential diary;
2. *a trusted adult*—as in a letter or even an assignment;
3. *a trusted friend of your own age*—as in a letter;
4. *yourself,* but with the knowledge that what you write will be *read by your teacher*—as in a journal that is handed in periodically;
5. *a teacher as partner*—as in a paper that you're glad to share, to which you may expect some reaction and comment but that will not be marked;
6. *a teacher as "master,"* when you understand that the teacher probably knows more than you do about writing and will "correct" the paper, probably MARK, 88 it, and suggest REVISIONS, 133 to help you write better;
7. *a teacher as examiner*—as in a test or exam, when you're writing to show how well you can and to get as good a mark as you can;
8. *your classmates*—as when you know that your paper may be read aloud by you or your teacher and may be discussed by the class or a group in the class, and your main task is to interest them;
9. *a public audience*—as when you write an article for the school paper or magazine or when you are assigned to write as if for the general public, whom you do not know personally.

Z

174. Zip codes

A zip code is a number that identifies each postal delivery area in the United States and some of its territories. The zip-code plan was started by the U.S. Post Office in 1963. The "zip" stands for "zone improvement plan." Be sure to use the zip code in all U.S. addresses you write. Recently, the Postal Service has developed a ZIP+4 Code (19138-1520) to ensure faster, more accurate delivery. You can find what your nine-figure zip code is by telephoning your local post office. (See LETTERS, 84 and STATE ABBREVIATIONS, 151.)

Index

This index gives *topic numbers,* not page numbers. The entries in CAPITAL LETTERS deal with subjects; the entries in *lowercase* (small) letters are words dealt with in the book. Look up a few entries and you'll get the idea.

Index

Index

Index

Index

Index

ERIC W. JOHNSON has taught English, social studies, and sex education to grades 5–12 for more than thirty years. A graduate of the Germantown Friends School in Philadelphia and Harvard College, he earned a M.A. in Teaching at the Harvard Graduate School of Education. He is the author or coauthor of more than fifty books (with over 21 million copies sold to date), including *Improve Your Own Spelling, You Are the Editor, How to Live Through Junior High School, Love and Sex in Plain Language, Love and Sex and Growing Up* and *Teaching School: Points Picked Up.*

Johnson, whose favorite activities include travel, writing, speedwalking, arguing, exchanging humorous stories, and being married to his wife of 42 years (the last being the most important), consults frequently with schools and continues to write books. He is a lifelong resident of Germantown, Philadelphia, except during World War II and the time he spent working with the American Friends Service Committee (Quakers).

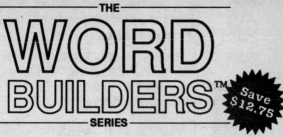